Praise for 1

"As a fellow Husky-wearing Southerner, I really relate to Dean's anecdotes. This book is filled with lessons to never forget."—Ryan Seacrest, Host of *American Idol*

"All the charm of Robert Fulghum…Good advice for anyone, and Johnson's musing offer soothing companionship along the way. As refreshingly southern and satisfying as a cool glass of iced tea."—*Kirkus Discoveries*

"Dean takes an honest, clean, forthright look at his past…as the book continues, we are introduced to friends and family, to feuds and feasts…we may laugh or cry, but more importantly, we may actually think, 'What is the meaning of life?'"—*Transitions News Magazine*

"It's a lot like Chicken Soup For the Southern Boy's Soul."—*Instinct Magazine*

"Dean has wisdom to impart. He loves life and it shows. This is a fun read!"—*Sandlapper Magazine*

"As refreshing as a glass of cold buttermilk sipped on a screened porch during a late-summer shower."—**Celia Rivenbark,** author of *We're Just Like You, Only Prettier* and *Bless Your Heart, Tramp*

"Out of all the stars in the Southern sky, this one stands out in pure, honest brilliance. Read it. Take its message to heart. Most importantly, live differently because of it."—**Deb Austin Brown,** author of *Lessons from the Beach Chair* and *Growing Character*

Life. Be There at Ten 'Til.

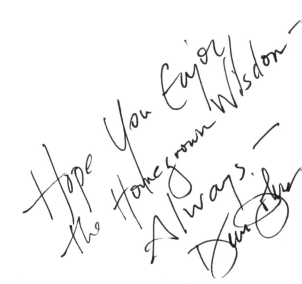

Life. Be There at Ten 'Til.

◆

A Collection of Homegrown Wisdom

R. Dean Johnson

iUniverse Star
New York Lincoln Shanghai

Life. Be There at Ten 'Til.
A Collection of Homegrown Wisdom

iUniverse Star
an iUniverse, Inc. imprint

iUniverse books may be ordered through booksellers or by contacting:

iUniverse
2021 Pine Lake Road, Suite 100
Lincoln, NE 68512
www.iuniverse.com
1-800-Authors (1-800-288-4677)

ISBN-13: 978-1-58348-232-2 (pbk)
ISBN-13: 978-0-595-79003-6 (ebk)
ISBN-10: 1-58348-232-6 (pbk)
ISBN-10: 0-595-79003-8 (ebk)

Printed in the United States of America

For

Daddy and Mama
(Robert B. and Shirley Dawsey Johnson)

Contents

Preface

I began observing and internalizing the world around me at an early age. I closely watched other people's behavior. I listened not only to what they said but how they said it. I heard what they didn't say. I noticed both subtle and overt gestures and mannerisms. Everything left an impression that has lasted all my life.

My mama, who was a schoolteacher for almost forty years, used to say that one reason I fared better than my older brother in school was because I was always watching over her shoulder while she was helping him with homework lessons. As a result, I was more academically prepared by the time I started first grade. Whether I had an advantage may or may not be true, but she is certainly right about one thing: I was always "looking over someone's shoulder," so to speak. I was, in fact, listening and watching. Always.

Without a doubt, it was my early, more formative years while growing up in the South where my family, my culture, and my world supplied a lifelong dose of humor, love, understanding, and sense of knowing. By carefully observing the world around me, I gained great insight into the nuances of human behavior. I retained tidbits of conversations, actions, events, joys, sorrows, and moments of everyday living. This over-the-shoulder education enabled me to identify, interpret, and embrace meaningful insights and life-affirming values. The significance of these insights and values is that I gained wisdom, homegrown wisdom, wisdom from my life and from those around me.

It is this wisdom I wish to share for many reasons. It is certainly a tribute to my parents, who gave unselfishly to my brother and me every day of their lives, and still do.

I also believe in sharing the wealth of wisdom. It would be an awful shame not to let others know that the greatest lessons in life come from the most simple and unsuspecting instances, moments, and situations. I encourage people to look for these lessons of life in every turn of the corner. Whether you're in line at the grocery store, sitting on a park bench, talking with your folks, or driving by the town clock. You never know what you'll discover—or when you'll discover it.

Wisdom gained through life is a blessing and treasure. It is unique and personal to each soul. It is different and yet the same, but it is worth capturing, experiencing, and internalizing. We are better and the the world is a better place when we *know*.

I share with you moments from my life that generated lessons learned and wisdom gained. Regardless of whether the story or situation took place last year or thirty years ago, the memory is as fresh today as when it occurred. For sure, each lesson is still fresh. Wisdom has an infinite shelf life.

Acknowledgments

Eternal thanks to Steven Shore for adamantly encouraging this humble writing initiative. With his support, the motivation to write was ever present. To Sybil Gleaton, my indebtedness for always encouraging self-expression and exploration. To Dawn James, generous thanks for helping package the final product while lending an arsenal of technical and creative resources. To Shannon Bogan, my gratitiude for seeing and believing a long time ago. To Tiffani Thiessen, a nod of honor and thanks for not only opening doors that I would have never been able to access, but for crossing the thresholds with me and walking by my side. To my brother Eric, a grateful reminder that you were there too—then and now. And to my parents, I dedicate this book as an extended and lifelong "thank you" note to show my immeasurable appreciation and love for the inspiration, patience, and support that enabled this creation.

Life. Be There.

"If a man tells me to meet him at the town clock at one o'clock, I'll be there at ten 'til..." So says my daddy, and I can't think of a better way to measure your character than by your ability to be on time, or by being there like you said you would.

Accountability is fast becoming a victim of modern-day conveniences. Cell phones, pagers, e-mail, voice mail, screen names, caller ID, caller ID blocking, and more have joined forces to help destroy humanity's sense of obligation and responsibility. I don't think that was their initial intention, but it may be time for the Hall of Justice to dispatch a team of superheroes who will fight the dismissive nature these technologies and services have evoked.

We have access to resources that enable the world to connect and communicate with rapid speed efficiency. We have every reason and opportunity to enjoy a bounty of Hallmark card moments. But we don't. Unless we want to or unless it's convenient. The problem isn't with modern age telecommunications. I guess we don't need super heroes to destroy this militia of devices and gadgets after all. It's not the town clock, but rather the man who doesn't show up at the town clock. The problem lies with us.

This is not an instance of the pot calling the kettle "black." I am as guilty as they come. Forgive me, Father, for I have sinned. I have let e-mails sit in my mailbox for days before acknowledging them with a response. Armed with caller ID on my cell phone, I have accepted or declined calls depending on my mood, my location, the time of day, the nature of the call (i.e., the caller), or the barometric pressure. In other words, I have screened phone calls. I have responded, or not, at my leisure. Why? I don't know. I simply don't know.

I do know that a rather dismissive, "throw-away" mentality seems to be making more and more public appearances as its campaign gathers steam. More than ever before, we quickly discard refuse, inconveniences, and situations that are no longer attractive or appealing—whether we're talking about Styrofoam or marriage. One is as easily disposable as the other.

Could it be that self-absorption has consumed us to the point that responsibility and accountability to people and to our environment are no longer important in defining our character? Perhaps people would rather be defined by the jobs they have, the company they keep, the clothes they wear, the homes they own, and the lifestyles they publicly maintain.

Have we become lazy? Maybe we just do what we want to do as opposed to what we should do. When I was in junior high school, I came home one afternoon, and Mama was taking a casserole dish out of the oven. Murk Brown, who lived up the road from us, had died. I didn't know much about Murk or his wife, Dolly, but they were neighbors nonetheless. They didn't regularly attend the little church in our community. I rarely saw them out in their yard, sitting on their porch, or working around their farm. I'm sure they did all these things; I know they did all these things. But, the few and far between spottings created mystery rather than familiarity. Their house sat back in the field away from the road, and they always seemed to be at a distance. As a result, they were people in our community of whom I had no knowledge or understanding. They were complete strangers to me. I didn't see any reason for Mama to be frying chicken and making macaroni and cheese casserole for this bereaved family. When I asked her why, she said, "Because it's what I'm *supposed* to do. Most people only do what they *want* to do." There was only one thing Mama could do: that which she was supposed to do.

I'm not completely sure why this collective consciousness toward dismissive behavior has evolved or how it happened exactly. It's almost like the pesky ten pounds I carry around. I woke up one day, and there they were. How? I repeat: I don't know. I simply don't know. But I wasn't raised to be dismissive of any sense of responsibility to my family, to my friends, to my community, or to the world around me. I wasn't raised to be unaccountable. I was raised with a sense of character. I was raised to be at the clock by ten 'til one.

During my childhood, if the phone rang at our house, it was answered. There was no caller ID or answering machine to help avoid certain callers. There was no call waiting. If you got a busy signal, you kept calling until you finally got someone on the line. When cars pulled up in the driveway, we raced to the window to see who was coming. We welcomed the intrusion. We didn't look through a peephole and act as if no one was home. Whether a neighbor or stranger, friend or foe, we answered. We answered calls, and we answered knocks at the door.

We were accountable. And you can bet that if the Johnson family was supposed to be somewhere at a certain time, they arrived early. Being where we were supposed to be and doing what we were supposed to do defined us both as a family and as individuals. We were there.

A popular t-shirt I recall from my college days simply read: *Life. Be In It.* Not only did I find the message profound, I was overwhelmed that so few words spoke such volume. Many years later, I was driving home with Daddy and we passed the town clock in downtown Conway, South Carolina. I was instantly reminded of what he had said a long time ago, and it occurred to me that my favorite t-shirt slogan of the 80's could stand a little retrofitting—perhaps a spin-off that reflects a more current directive. And so, I offer these words of wisdom: Life. Be There At 10 'Til.

Creatures of Habit

Day in and day out, our lives become a pattern of familiar habits and chores. We drive the same route to work. We come home, go to the gym, eat dinner, watch our favorite television shows, talk with friends on the phone, and go to bed. Each day becomes a replica of the one before. We thrive on consistency, and many times deviations from the routine occur only at the initiative of life itself—not through any conscious effort of our own.

And what's wrong with a little monotony here or a little mundaness there? Hardly anything because there is so much comfort and solace in the familiarity of routines—in what we know versus what we don't know. We thrive on predictability, and, on those occasions when we begin to feel complacent or restless due to the "same old same old," we are acutely reminded that the same routines we complain about are the very same ones we cherish when they no longer exist.

A story of a dog named Lum fondly reminds me that, not only are we all God's creatures, but we are also his creatures of habit.

Years and years ago, my paternal grandparents, George O. and Tronie Johnson, acquired two male puppies from a litter of newborns. My daddy was just a small boy when the puppies were brought home. The two dogs were very different looking and in no way favored each other. They were named Lum and Abner. (For those not familiar with the golden age of radio, Lum Edwards and Abner Peabody were two popular on-air

personalities who starred in a daily comedy serial appropriate-
ly named "Lum 'n Abner.") My grandparents kept Lum, and
Abner was given to another relative.

Lum led a surprisingly sedentary lifestyle considering he was a
farm dog. All he did was sleep and "waller" (the Southern pro-
nunciation for wallow) in a hole he dug out by the side of my
grandparents' house. His primary source of physical activity
came when it was time to eat. It was then that he would leave his
hole. After the meal, it was back to the shade and his hole in the
ground. Day in and day out, nothing ever changed until the day
when Granddaddy George got tired of feeding and looking after
a farm dog who wouldn't scratch the fleas on his back, let alone
run a chicken on the farmyard. Lum soon became the property
of Mr. Kit Lewis, who lived on the Waccamaw River in the nearby town of Conway, South Carolina.

There was no cruelty or harm intended by gifting Lum to
someone else. After all, Mr. Kit was a friend of the family, and
his home was just yards away from where my grandparents
would go fishing on the Waccamaw River. It was on a visit to
see Mr. Kit that Granddaddy George asked him if he would be
interested in owning a good dog—a lazy dog, but a good dog.
Mr. Kit was interested, and Lum had a new home.

Some months later, my grandparents decided to catch some
fish for supper. They hitched a paddle boat to the truck and
headed to Conway and the fishing landing near Mr. Kit's property. To access the river's landing, they drove down a narrow
dirt road that passed directly by his house.

When Granddaddy George drove by, Lum knew the sound
of the truck and recognized the visitors. He followed them to
the landing, where he greeted them affectionately. Once reac-
quainted with their former pet, my grandparents proceeded to

put the boat in the water and head down the river to fish. When they returned a few hours later, Lum was in the truck, sitting proudly in the middle of the seat. How he got there, no one knew exactly. The doors to the truck had been closed, although the windows had been left open.

Upon seeing Lum in the truck seat, Granddaddy George said to Lum, "Well, if you want to come home that damn bad, I'll take ya," and on the ride back home, Lum generously thanked them as he licked one and then the other for the duration of the drive.

As my grandparents pulled into the driveway, Lum jumped out of the truck and ran to the side of the house where he proceeded to dig out his old hole. He then lay down in it and went to sleep. He slept until it was time to eat, and, after his welcome-home meal, it was back to the comfort of his hole—to his routine and his life. Where he belonged.

The process of change is important and necessary. For humanity, change is what allows us to grow—to embrace and internalize such wonderful qualities as wisdom, awareness, humility, and love. For mankind, change advances such fields as technology and medicine to previously unimaginable degrees of skill and expertise so that our quality of life is immeasurably improved. We would perish if change did not touch our lives in some way.

But there are times when a little bit goes a long way. Although change is a good thing, it is constancy and familiarity that feed our souls and nourish our spirits. That which enables us to realize and grasp wisdom, awareness, humility, and love is also that which we see, hear, taste, smell, and do on a daily basis.

If we creatures of habit ever step beyond the familiar and into the unknown, there is comfort in knowing our routines await our return should we find the unfamiliar less than what we expected or desired. All of God's creatures have familiar holes along the side of a house. Holes to which we can return to if necessary. Where we can waller in comfort.

Birthday Girls

It's Saturday morning. When I woke up, the first thing I did was return Daddy's phone call from the night before. It's not that he had left a message on the answering machine, but he always tries to catch me at home on Friday nights. The phone will ring three times before the machine clicks on, and then the caller hangs up. That's Daddy calling.

Leaving a message would mean waiting for the beep, remembering what buttons to press, and wondering whether his message was actually recorded. When my roommate told me that someone kept calling and hanging up last night, I knew what my priority of this Saturday morning would be.

So I call Daddy back, knowing full well the first thing that will be asked: "Where were you last night?" Whether I might be at home screening calls or actually unavailable to take the call is not a consideration. I answer the question, as always, with my own question: "Why didn't you leave a message?" And he always responds, "I ain't leavin' no message on some machine."

Daddy reported to me the usual "goin's-on." He had just come from the garden and had picked enough peanuts so he and Mama could boil "a mess" later in the evening. The weather was sunny. They had thunderstorms and some afternoon rain showers last week. He added, "Ya' mama's gettin' ready to go out to your Aunt Doe's for a birthday party."

Aunt Doe (short for Trevejo—a Brazilian name that was suggested by relatives who were missionaries in South America) is a retired nurse who is now in her mid-eighties. She lives in the small town of Aynor, South Carolina, where she, my mother, and their brothers and sisters were all born. It's a little community with a population of around seven hundred people and is located about ten minutes from the farm where my parents live. During her lifetime, Aunt Doe has suffered, endured, and survived so many challenges including divorce, the diagnosis of cancer, a mastectomy, several strokes, a car accident, and the loss of her oldest son when he was in the prime of his life. And now, all the new ailments that old age generously affords are in pursuit. The decline of her mental faculties is leading this charge. Daddy says she just sits and stares a lot of the time. Mama concurs. And with a sense of resignation that life is nearing its end for her sister, she comments, "I think Doe knows me, but sometimes I wonder if she even remembers I come by to see about her."

As I hear the stories of Aunt Doe's progressive decline, it's hard to believe this is the same woman who taught me how to swim when I was fifteen years old. It only seems like it was last summer that my cousin Harley and I went to Bagnal's drugstore and bought her a gold-plated pendant. It was 1978 and her birthday. We spent the night with Aunt Doe, but we didn't get a lot of sleep. She snored all night as we lay awake laughing. We tried to sneak into her room to watch her, but every time we got close, we seemed to step on just the right spot in the hallway where the boards creaked. She would immediately wake up and say, "I hear you, boys. What are you up to?"

But on this Saturday morning, Daddy says the "ladies" (home health aides) who stay with her around the clock are having a little party for her birthday, and Mama is going.

As I listen to Daddy, I can see Mama standing in front of the mirror, brushing her white hair, and getting ready to go. It won't take her but a minute. She may smear on a little lipstick (that's how Mama says it), but I doubt it. Mama has never been one to fuss over her appearance. She doesn't wear perfume or makeup, although she does keep a little compact in the top drawer of her bureau. I've seen her dust her face with the powder puff only a handful of times in my life. And, it's about once a year that she goes to Corlous' Beauty Shop to have her hair fixed. Specifically, she gets a permanent. But that's all.

She's never been particular about her wardrobe. A few sets of polyester slacks and matching tops occupy her closet. She has a limited collection of frocks that she would have reason to wear. She's very simple in her appearance, but nonetheless striking.

I can see her driving alone, by herself, along the country highway that leads to my aunt's house, attending to her responsibility and duty as a sister.

There will probably be a cake in honor of my aunt's birthday. Soft drinks will be served. Maybe there will be a bowl of punch. And it wouldn't be a gathering in the South if someone didn't make a homemade cheese ball to serve with crackers. The ladies who help take care of Aunt Doe and a handful of friends or relatives will sit around and make small talk with Mama. "She ate a real good supper last night and seemed to understand everything I talked about," one might be heard saying. Another will add, "I think I might try and get her in the car and take her over to Wal-Mart tomorrow if she feels all right." After about an hour, Mama will leave. The party will be over.

Later in the same day, it's early evening on the West Coast, and I'm driving to a birthday dinner in Los Angeles for my friend Lesley. At about this same time back on the East Coast, Aunt Doe has probably been tucked into bed, and, hopefully, she will soon sleep.

Reservations for the birthday engagement I'm attending were made at a noted Italian restaurant in Burbank. During the course of the evening, we dined at a beautifully set table and enjoyed a delicious meal. We toasted the occasion with really good wine. We talked about our jobs. We talked about movies. We talked about politics. We talked about our lives. We took photographs. We smiled and laughed.

When dinner was over, I walked outside and gazed at the mountains that line the San Fernando Valley. I looked at the stars in the sky. I felt the summer breeze brush across my face. A chill came over me, and I thought about Aunt Doe. What was she seeing in her dreams this same night? Did she see mountains and stars? Did she feel the wind? Was she dreaming of heaven?

Two women I know celebrated birthdays this day. They are two very different women with very different lives. They are separated by distance, by time, by cultures, and by life experiences. They are worlds apart, but there is a thread of commonality. They are both women I know and am glad to have known. And they both celebrated their lives this day, albeit in very different ways.

Birthdays not only honor the gift of life we have been given on earth, but they also mark the passing of life. One day, these birthday girls will not be in my life. The passage of time will acknowledge the circle of life as other birthday girls, in other cultures, in other places, and in other times celebrate both the birth and passing of their own lives—differently, and yet in the same way.

"Ya' mama's gettin' ready to go out to your Aunt Doe's for a birthday party." I'm glad I called Daddy this morning and was reminded to celebrate life.

* Aunt Doe (Trevejo Dawsey Fore) passed away September 22, 2002. She is missed.

A Cedar Chest and a Cubbyhole

Mama and Daddy don't use the attic anymore. Everything from the artificial Christmas tree to our old Rock'em, Sock'em Robots is now carefully packed away in a modern storage shed that boasts vinyl siding and decorative trim. It's all very designer-friendly, considering this shed sits out behind their house and close to the edge of the woods—designer-friendly, considering all you want is to have a place to put old, artificial flower arrangements and out-of-style bedspreads. Compared to years ago, the storage capabilities have significantly changed. Even the dirty clothes hamper in their hallway bathroom now doubles as a cabinet for household paper products and bathroom toiletries. You'll find no dirty underwear in what was once an under-the-cabinet roll-out unit. The keepsakes that once adorned our home and hearth now seem incongruently tucked away in less cherished and more sterile, although more attractive, confines. Many years before, our few belongings were stored in a cedar chest and cubbyhole—the heart and soul of our little house in South Carolina. And now, the memory of the cedar chest and cubbyhole are safely kept in my heart and soul.

Growing up in South Carolina, my immediate family consisted of my parents, Robert B. (Bobby) Johnson and Shirley Dawsey Johnson, my older brother, Eric, and me. We lived in a tiny house on a tobacco farm in a rural community. One side of the house consisted of two bedrooms that were connected by a tiny bathroom. The other side of the house was composed of a kitchen and small den. A table sat in the kitchen and represented our dining area. We had only one small closet. A screened-in porch adorned the front of the house, and a dirt floor carport was attached to the back. The carport was actually a shed that extended from the roof at the back of the house. Still, it was a carport. My parents always made sure there was pine straw to cover the dirt floor in order to cut down on the dust when the car was pulled under the shed. If you walked out the back door of the house, you were always greeted with the smell of fresh pine.

I suppose there wasn't anything particularly special about the house. It wasn't fancy, but it was clean. Mama made sure of that. And it was our "stay place" as my daddy might say. "Stay place" always appealed to me as a name for calling one's house, "home." The phrase evoked a certain sense of ownership and belonging. If anything, a stay place helped define who you were. The first time I heard my daddy use the phrase, I had an immediate understanding of what it meant to lay claim to something.

We had a white pit bull named Cheebie. Anytime another dog would wander up or "take up" at our house looking for scraps, Cheebie would defend her territory, and a fight would ensue. If we ever came home after dark, the headlights from the car would illuminate both the house and the woods behind the house as the car came down the driveway. Cheebie would take off running through the woods the moment the car lights hit the house. She was in attack mode as if she was chasing off intruders or potential squatters from the animal kingdom. By the time we had parked the car, you could hear Cheebie running through the dark woods headed back to the house to greet us. Limbs and branches would be breaking and popping. Leaves would be crunching. She was ready to see us. Daddy would always say, "This is her stay place. She ain't gonna have nothin' upsettin' it."

So our first little stay place with five rooms had nothing that was extraordinary by most standards, but to a child that is three or four years old, simple things assumed the illusion of something very grand. As an adult, I now look back on so much of my childhood and view people, places, and things with a more grown-up perspective that dispels the once-perceived magic. As we move through life, we hopefully have the opportunity to not only know more wonderful moments and experiences, but to own and enjoy material possessions that we only dreamed of as children. But regardless of where I travel, who I meet, the restaurants I enjoy, or the things I buy, my mind still retains the magic and wonder of two things that our simple house in South Carolina had: a cedar chest and a cubbyhole.

In the bedroom where I slept, a large cedar chest sat at the foot of the bed. It was only on occasion that Mama would open it. It was never locked, but I never felt privileged enough to attempt an entry. The few times it was opened, I was always captivated by an assortment of things that I thought were priceless and rare. It contained Daddy's athletic block letter from his high school letterman jacket. Mama's college diploma sat safely inside. There were a couple of photo albums with pictures from Daddy's time spent in Korea as a member of the U.S. Air Force, and there was also a collection of blankets. When the chest was opened, the smell of cedar filled the room. I somehow knew that the things inside were from my parents' lives before they were married and before my brother and I were born. The concept of their lives together before having had children was not something I could easily imagine.

My belief was that in this cedar chest, which sat in this simple farmhouse, some great mystery of life existed. Within the cedar chest was also a solution to the mystery, a mystery that was far greater and more significant than my own family. Maybe this mystery would be told when we were older. But, whatever mystical assimilation I made, it was special. *I was living with something special in my house.*

Facing the cedar chest were two shelves built high up on the wall. Mama had pinned a curtain over the shelving so nothing would be exposed. We called it "the cubbyhole." It was just shelves covered by a curtain, but it too was magical. Linen, towels, pillows, and maybe some clothes were kept there due to our lack of storage space. Everything in the cubbyhole smelled differently. The fragrance of laundry detergent was prevalent. A smell associated with things that are new or unused fueled my belief that everything stored inside was reserved for special occasions. Because it was a rarity for Mama to extract anything from this ingenious shelving unit, I was always convinced that company must be coming to visit or something very special was going to happen when she did.

The sight of her fumbling behind the curtains for something was reason enough to spend the day wondering with excitement. In a tiny house with no ornate finishes or master design, the cubbyhole was a world of excitement. It could have been the eighth wonder of the world. Its design was an architectural feat to behold. Who would have ever thought to mask the shelves with a curtain?

Years later, we eventually moved into a bigger house built by Daddy. This new home was basically constructed in the front yard of the old house—an almost shameless display of one-upmanship. And quietly, the little house graciously stepped aside as she would no longer be in need of service. It was months after we moved in when I took notice of the cedar chest's whereabouts. In the large walk-in closet of my parents bedroom sat the wood box. Alone and in the dark. With lots of shelves, cabinets and storage space, the chest had little to do other than sit in silence. I then realized that without curtains pinned to the shelving, a cubbyhole no longer existed at all. The prominence of both the cedar chest and cubbyhole had been lessened by more modern conveniences.

Fast-forward thirty years. Today, as I was placing suitcases and boxes into the luxurious, designer storage unit in Mama and Daddy's backyard, I raised an eyebrow to its assuming functionality. I returned its mightier-than-thou attitude with a fond remembrance of the cedar chest and cubbyhole. I reminded this unit of what my life was like in a tiny house not much bigger than it. But, the tiny house I reference was special—unlike this proud peacock with vinyl siding. Our house was simple and real. It provided memories of a good life. The new kid on the new cement blocks got the message.

To a small child who knew very little about the world, I did know that in the most plain and unassuming circumstances or situations there is always something that can capture your heart if you allow it. The first time I flew in a private jet, I was headed to Hawaii for a work-related project. As I sat looking out the window of the plane, I thought about my childhood, and I thought about the cubbyhole and cedar chest. It seemed as though I had come a long way from watching Mama pull back the curtain of the cubbyhole or open the lid of the cedar chest, but in an instant of wishful thinking, I wanted to be a child again. I wanted to smell the aroma of cedar as the chest was opened. I wanted to be there as she fumbled behind the curtain of the cubbyhole in search of whatever.

Though we can't go back in time, I am glad to know that wherever I go or whatever I do, *I've always held and will always hold the capacity to appreciate and value that which is simple.* Magic and happiness are timeless. I knew magic and happiness as a child and I appreciate such emotions as an adult because they stem from *simplicity*—not monetary value or vintage status. But, the cedar chest and cubbyhole both held value and status in my heart and mind. They made me feel safe. They made me feel special. They made me feel rich. They still do.

Stars and Eggs

Childhood fantasies and imaginations have come a long way. All I wanted to do in 1971 was sneak up on Santa Claus and ask whether he would let me go back to the North Pole with him. I had a plan already in place. You see, Mama and Daddy wouldn't mind. Mrs. Claus and I would call them just as soon as Santa and I got back to the castle. Silly, huh? I was neither goal-oriented nor imaginative compared to the wish lists of these more hi-tech times. How ridiculous to think that a one-year hiatus with Santa could compare to the juvenile aspirations of today—aspirations that probably involve commando operatives, extreme sports stars, and PlayStation masterminds. But whatever short-lived fantasy I had regarding Santa (and it ended sometime around 1977, when I learned the truth), one childhood visual remained eternal and life defining: the visual of a starry night along with the smell of scrambled eggs.

One of the most frequently asked questions during a job interview is, what makes you qualified for the position? I had always been prepared to answer this question with a standard, rote response, such as, "Well, I'm a team player, and your organization certainly seems to be an environment that supports a spirit of cooperation." Or better yet, "The job is one that offers the professional opportunities I have long desired to pursue." Like most applicants, I was prepared to tell prospective employers what I thought they wanted to hear. However, the first time I ever interviewed for a job as a celebrity personal assistant in Los Angeles and was asked the question du jour, I answered honestly and without hesitation. My response painted a clear picture of my character, which I inherited completely from my parents. And while the response came from my heart, its technical origin was the seat of my daddy's Ford pickup truck, where my brother and I lay sleeping one early summer morning in 1966.

Daddy was a farmer. During the fall, he harvested corn and soybeans. But during the summer, tobacco crops took center stage. Farming tobacco was (and still is) a time-sensitive process that began with planting very tiny tobacco seeds in the early winter. The seeds would then grow into small plants that would be hand picked by late winter or early spring. Next, these hand-pulled plants were immediately transplanted in the fields. By early summer, the tobacco plants grew into full stalks of firm green leaves that were ready for harvesting (the process of removing the leaves from the stalks). Once harvested, the leaves were mounted on sticks using twine and then hung in barns. The barns were equipped with large burners, much like an oven, in order to bake the leaves to a golden brown. This baking process was referred to as "curing the tobacco." Farming tobacco was hard work that required the help of a large crew of workers, especially when it came time to begin the harvesting process. (Today's tobacco farmers have the advantage of more advanced farm machinery and more sophisticated equipment, which have replaced certain aspects of the manual labor requirement.)

As was the case throughout our little Southern farming community, the crew of laborers used to help "gather" (i.e., harvest) the tobacco most often included black people looking to find work in the summer. We referred to the black labor force as "hands." Daddy used to wake up way before sunrise and drive to neighboring towns to pick up the hands. When he returned, it was daybreak and time to start work.

Labor was expensive, and when you're trying to make any kind of money from farming, family members do as much of the work themselves in order to insure any level of profit. Both Daddy and Mama worked endlessly to reduce as much labor expense as possible. As an adult, I can only imagine how tired they must have been at the end of a day. I do know where they found the strength. From their own childhoods and their own parents. Hard work was just a way of life they had always known. There was no other choice but to do whatever was necessary to get the job done.

Mama was also a schoolteacher. She came home each day after school in the winter and spring to do what she could to help with the farmwork. This was in addition to cooking, cleaning, washing clothes, and taking care of my brother and me. During the summer, she became a full-time farmhand herself. Daddy hardly ever slept during the summer, as he lay awake at night worrying about whether the hired hands would show up for work. He worried that the crops were doomed due to lack of rain. And once the tobacco was curing in the barns, he was up and down during the middle of most nights, double-checking temperatures and burners to make sure the curing process was proceeding as it should.

In the South, people who live on farms work hard. They're not the kind of farms that the rich and famous aspire to own. The farms I knew as a child were working farms run by working people. Days spent in the sun and in the fields take a toll on a body. When I return home to visit these days, I notice how much differently people look in terms of physical health. They look weathered and appear far older than they should. I'm convinced their accelerated aging has much to do with the level of physical exertion and the nature of farmwork.

By the time my brother and I were big enough to begin helping on the farm, I'm not so sure we were that much help to Mama and Daddy. We did our share, but they took many extra steps to avoid having us do it. Over and over, they worked so we wouldn't have to work. I suppose that most children would have been spoiled by not learning the value of hard work, but nothing my parents ever did went unnoticed. They were nurturers and providers of the most extreme kind. I actually think it worked to our advantage. My brother and I are both committed and loyal employees in our respective professions. We have tremendous work ethics. We are both providers, and we are both nurturers. We learned by example.

My first memory of my parents' willingness to take extra steps in providing for their children was probably around the time I was three years old. Eric and I were awakened in the very early hours of a summer morning, while it was still very dark outside. Mama and Daddy were going to the tobacco field to work, and they were taking us with them. Their mission this particular morning was to begin "topping" the tobacco. It helps to know that tobacco stalks eventually sprout a huge blossom at the top of the stalk. This blossom must be removed, or "topped off," in order for the stalks' leaves to fully develop. Fully developed leaves, once cured, bring a better price at the market when it's time to sell the tobacco. Topping each individual stalk was done by hand in those days. Only years later were machines available to take care of this tedious, laborious, and lengthy aspect of tobacco farming.

Since the days were so hot and humid, it just made sense to work in the early morning hours, while it was still dark and the temperatures were much cooler. Plus, any amount of work my parents could do on their own was that much more they didn't have to spend paying the hands to work. After waking us, they put us in the pickup truck and drove to one of the tobacco fields located behind a large pinewood forest. My brother and I were left in the truck, and my parents worked in the dark field. We were wrapped in blankets. Mama and Daddy kept stopping by the truck to check on us. At times, I woke up, and all I could see were the stars in the sky. I could faintly hear the sound of tobacco tops breaking from the stalks. I could hear my parents talking to each other, and I could smell the scrambled egg sandwiches wrapped tightly in tinfoil. Mama had made breakfast so there would be something to eat in case we woke up and were hungry.

At the time, I wasn't particularly clear on what exactly was happening in the field and why we were in the pickup truck in the middle of the night, but I knew I was safe and being cared for. I instinctively knew that my parents were doing something to make our lives better. What they don't know is *how* it made our lives better.

It wasn't enough that they were always sacrificing in so many ways to provide for our family. Their actions were instructional. We learned the art of absolute selflessness. The curriculum was grounded in the act of giving and not receiving. The ability to nurture, care, and love was developed through hands-on training. People never know the gifts they give by actions alone. We always had food on the table and clean clothes to wear. There was nothing especially extravagant that we owned in terms of material possessions. We never had fancy cars. We rarely went on vacations. But we lived a simple life that was rich, and, most importantly, we were schooled to unselfishly put other's needs ahead of our own.

Little did I know that I was accumulating the ability and instinct needed to work in a profession as a celebrity assistant, where I must be proactive, be prepared, think on my feet, be resourceful, be selfless, be constantly aware, be mentally and physically strong, be tolerant, and be committed. In essence, to be a parent and guardian. As a result, when I was asked why I would be qualified for the job of personally assisting a celebrity, my mind went back in time to the night I lay wrapped in a blanket in an old pickup truck.

My response was based on a lifetime of examples my parents had set: *"All I have ever known is what it is like to be cared for. I have been expertly trained in the ability to provide for and to nurture. My entire life has been a lesson in caring for the needs of others in the most dedicated and tireless of ways."* The job was mine. I take great pride in the answer I gave that day.

The fantasy of living at the North Pole seemed exciting. But, what would it have done for me? I mean, really? However, the childhood memory of a starry night and the smell of scrambled eggs shaped my life in the most admirable and noble of ways.

Growing Up in Payless

We all have defining moments—those moments in time when a wealth of understanding, sense of knowing, and insight pass through us, refashion our psyche, and leave us far more in tune with the world than we could have imagined. We remember these personal moments much like some of the great historical events we've learned in school. The difference between the two? One changes man, and the other changes mankind. Textbooks will continue to recount the Boston Tea Party, the ride of Paul Revere, Sherman's march during the Civil War, the assassinations of the Kennedys and King, flights into space, walks on the moon, wars and rumors of war, and even the day Elvis Presley died, but they will never reference the day I grew up in Payless ShoeSource. Nevertheless, it was a defining moment for me. It was the first time my daddy asked me to tie his shoes. And with that request, life began to change as I saw my future more as the caretaker and less the child. I grew up rather quickly in only a matter of seconds.

We know our parents as providers. We see them as pillars of strength. We seek comfort from them. We seek their guidance. We expect them to forever remain the safety net should we stumble and fall, but the passage of time and circle of life bring sobering news to those of us who have enjoyed the role of child. Our parents will grow old. They will weaken. They will come to depend on us, and we will assume the role of provider. It is the children who will evolve into pillars of strength. The once parents will seek comfort and guidance from the former child. We, as caretakers, will cast safety nets should they stumble and fall. And while this comes as no surprise to anyone, it is still a defining moment that happens when we least expect it. And the moment is as memorable and unforgettable as any other in our lives.

Aisle seven in the Payless ShoeSource at Columbiana Centre in Columbia, South Carolina, was designed to accommodate those men wearing size eleven and twelve shoes. From sandals and slippers to wing tips and loafers, practically every design and style of shoe was available for almost $29.99. For one dollar more, a second pair made the purchase double the fun. Who could beat a deal like that? Two pair of shoes for $30.99? And amid the promotional whoopla, a pair of brown, lace-up dress shoes appeared out of nowhere. Daddy, who had found a cushioned bench in the center of aisle seven had also discovered this "Johnny-come-lately" pair of brown lace-ups and was struggling to get them on his feet. He's older; he's heavier; he's not as limber; and he was struggling. He turned and saw me staring. "Can you help me slide these shoes on and tie them for me?" My life changed. He needed help tying his shoes—my help, his child's help.

It seems that it was just yesterday when a pair of saddle oxfords, ordered from the Sears and Roebuck catalogue, arrived via the mail. On second thought, it was 1968, and I had seen a Charlie Brown cartoon for the very first time. Charlie and all his friends—Linus, Lucy, Schroeder, and Peppermint Patty—all wore saddle oxfords, and I wanted a pair too. The shoes arrived, and I remember Daddy helping me tie them as I had no idea how to lace the strings and maneuver the knot. However, I knew that my work was cut out for me. I had to learn to tie those shoes. But until this learning curve was mastered, I had Mama and Daddy to help me—to resolve the challenge.

And now, almost thirty years later, Daddy was seeking my help. He needed me to help resolve his challenge.

I knew the tide would begin to change from this day forward. The parent-child relationship would begin a gradual role reversal process. I prayed it would be slow in coming. I still needed time to remain the child for as long as possible. I wasn't ready to be the guardian or caretaker anytime soon. I wasn't ready for my father to acknowledge his decline, regardless of how slight it might be. I feared the unknown. I began to envision a future in which his physical and mental deterioration would necessitate dependence on my brother or me for round-the-clock care. Would he get to the point where he could no longer feed himself? Would he have to be cared for like a child is cared for? If so, would he be less my Daddy and more my responsibility? Fear swept through me. The image of my father as a strong and virile man was one that I held on to with great emotional dependence. I didn't want this image to tarnish. I helped him with the shoes and tied them for him without speaking a word. He didn't like how they looked after all. They were left on the shelf. He walked out empty-handed. I didn't. I had gained a new sense of self.

It wasn't long after that day in Payless that I was home visiting my parents, when I felt that fear sweep through me again. Something on the bathroom counter caught my eye. Behind the soap dispenser on the vanity was a dirty spot of water that had not been wiped clean. My mother, known for keeping a house so clean that it's worthy of any impromptu white glove test, had missed a spot behind the dispenser. How could she miss something so obvious? Was her eyesight declining? Was her attention to detail less enthusiastic than it once was? She left an indelible reminder for me. No amount of Clorox and scrubbing would ever erase that spot of dirty water.

What was happening to my parents? One needs help tying his shoes, and the other missed a spot while wiping the counter! I looked in the mirror and experienced Payless déjà vu. There wasn't a song playing on the radio to mark the moment. No history book would ever detail the circumstances under which I felt transformed. The world would move on and time would soon pass. Somehow, I would learn to accept this much-dreaded passing of the baton as we shifted roles. More than anything, I would never forget the moment when I first realized this change had been set in motion.

Wars have since been fought. World leaders have both emerged and died. My parents are now grandparents. The death of Elvis Presley is still mourned, Payless ShoeSource store has new promotions, and a new soap dish sits on the counter in my old childhood bathroom. But one historical fact remains unchanged: though I was born and raised in Horry County in the great state of South Carolina, I really grew up in Payless ShoeSource.

Can You Dig It?

My mother's life has never been about bells and whistles. Embellishment and adornment have seldom occupied her thoughts. Extravagance has never been her need or desire. Attention and admiration have been deliberately avoided. Instead, she is a simple woman. And selfless. Her life has been quietly devoted to everyone but herself. I find that to be quite noble. She is noble. She is honorable. Dignity is the pedigree to which she is entitled. In a time when the world boasts leaders galore, there's not a head of state, king, queen, prince, princess, president, or first lady whose nobility or majesty is greater than my mama's. She's led a clean life and championed the virtues of clean underwear. She has given to others while seldom receiving. She's known loss without discovery. And all the while, she's maintained a sense of grace, acceptance, and steadfast poise. She is dignified. Define majesty and greatness any way you want. I say it's less about titles, treasures, and tiaras. Rather, it's about dignity. And at the end of the day, isn't that what we all aspire to have? Can you dig it?

Mama taught school in Horry County for just over forty years. People in practically every profession, from doctors to dentists to musicians to missionaries, represent the students she taught. And I can bet that all of these students know their multiplication tables. I already know two that do—my brother and

I. Students saw her as not only a teacher, but as a disciplinarian, a parental figure, a friend, and a mentor, but her work didn't end when the school bell rang at the end of the day. Once home, her second shift began as she cleaned, cooked, took clothes off the line, raked yards, ironed clothes, packed them away and washed more clothes while rarely taking time for herself. And come spring and summer, the role of farmer was assumed. She went from the classroom to the tobacco fields while helping Daddy with every aspect of the farm. It came as no surprise that when it was time for bed, she slept. She should have slept. She was tired—every day, every month, every season, every year.

As all good things must come to an end, so came the day when Mrs. Johnson, Horry Elementary School's third grade teacher, announced that she would retire. Her decision came within weeks of just having started a new academic year. She would not complete the full school year, but would leave when the district closed for the Christmas and New Year's holidays. I'm not satisfied with the circumstances that influenced her decision to retire from teaching. She was under the administrative watch of a new principal that particular year—a young and upwardly mobile principal by all accounts. He represented the vanguard of new teaching. As such, I'm not convinced that he appreciated her old-fashioned methods. Teaching seemed to be becoming less about teaching and more about strict methodologies, detailed planning, and documentation. She had earned a reputation for making students toe the line. She was demanding. She wasn't lenient. And most of us are grateful for having learned more than the three Rs under her tutelage.

We were exposed to a work ethic that was model behavior. We were taught a sense of responsibility and accountability. We were taught manners. We learned to be gracious. We learned the history of South Carolina. And every student got a valentine in his or her brown paper sack that was tacked to the wall come February 14. No one was left off the list. We learned many, many things seldom included in text books. Yet despite her years of service to education and to the families and students in our community, this principal would neither sing her praise nor note her tenure as golden. And one afternoon she came home and cried. Daddy told me. And so she decided to retire early.

On her last day of school, my brother and I took a day off from our jobs to drive home and be with her at school. We surprised her by joining her for lunch in the very same cafeteria ("the lunch room") we had frequented so many times and so many years before. While standing in line for my tray, I recalled my Aunt Ruth (not really my aunt, but a distant relative of my family) who used to manage the the lunch room. Aunt Ruth drove a silver, two-door Chevrolet Impala and smoked cigars. She arrived at school most mornings with the window down, a cigar stuck in the corner of her mouth, and a trail of dust following her to the lunch room's side entrance. She also made the best mashed potatoes and fried sausage patties I had ever tasted. As I would pass through the lunch line to get my tray, she would, on occasion, cleverly hide an extra pattie under my mound of potatoes. And upon my discovery, I would glance across the room and find her staring at me. I would smile, and she would wink.

Today there would be no extra pattie. No mashed potatoes. No bells and whistles for Mama. She was ending her teaching career without celebration or incident. My heart was broken. At the very least, surely there would be someone from the county office to present her a certificate. A gold watch? A pen? A word of thanks? Nothing. It wasn't customary to do so. And what about the principal who had found her to be antiquated and ready for pasture? He was nowhere to be found. I often wonder what example he serves to students wherever he may be. Courage and character are hard to come by. Maybe he would have been better served having been a student in Mrs. Shirley Johnson's third grade class.

My brother was as enraged as I, but we spoke not a word. Nor did my mother. Of course, she wouldn't have. She was too dignified to give credence to the obvious slight. She would have perished for lack of recognition rather than utter one word of deprivation. She would complete her last day of school without pomp and circumstance. And when the final bell rang, not only had another day ended, but a significant chapter in my mother's life was concluded.

I was relieved to know, on some level, that the other teachers (sans principal) had joined together in a small room inside the auditorium area where an almost clandestine moment of congratulations and farewell was bid. As they each sipped their punch and ate a piece of sheet cake, they were solemn. They spoke not a word of the conditions or circumstances that created this less-than-celebratory situation, but each person thanked her. They were grateful to her. We all were. We all should be. She represented an era of educators who were on the verge of extinction. A new wave of teachers under the influence of new instructional protocols were taking the reigns in shaping the minds of the future. And quietly, they all said their good-byes.

Mama then walked that long empty hallway to her retirement. Her steps echoed on the hardwood floors that Mamie Ellerbe, the school custodian for as long as I can remember, had waxed that very day. I found the sheen and luster from the floor to be a red carpet of sorts. Perhaps it was Mamie's tribute to my mother.

As she walked, I saw the image of two little boys run up behind her carrying their books and begging to know what she would be fixin' for supper. She replied, "I don't know 'til I get home. I got to take the clothes in off the line and wash two more loads. Ya' daddy said we might have to reset some tobacco plants." Her day wasn't over. There was more work to do once she got home. If she was tired, she wouldn't say a word. She endured what was necessary and went about the day doing what needed to be done. And when bedtime came, she would sleep. She should. She would be tired.

As we all drove away from Horry Elementary School on my mother's day of retirement, I felt as though the world may never know what Mama had contributed throughout her career—perhaps her life. She never did anything with the hope or expectation of thanks or praise. I am reminded that sometime after her sister, my Aunt Rog (short for Roger Lee) passed away, Rog's one and only son suffered a stroke and was placed in a rehab center. The son, Gene, never recovered. He didn't know he was in the world. He didn't know his family, let alone his name, but Mama would visit him and take him a pack of crackers and a soft drink. She would leave his goodies sitting on a side table. She would say, "I reckon he gets his goodies. But it won't matter if he does or doesn't. As long I brought him something." She would often take clippers and trim his fingernails and toenails. She did it for Aunt Rog's memory as much as she did it for Gene himself. Regardless of his condition and hope for recovery, he was Rog's son and her nephew. He mattered. Whether anyone knew what she did for Gene was of no concern to her. It was about dignity—her dignity, Rog's dignity, Gene's dignity.

The world now knows that my mother's life has been about unrecognized service and giving. I have personally seen to that, and it's well-overdue. She embodies a state of grace and unassuming beauty that is majestic and great. Dignity is not reserved just for the dignitaries. It defines so many people in the world who are selfless and sacrificing without recognition—from third world countries to third grade classrooms.

At the end of the day, all that many people ever really have is their dignity. At the end of the day, isn't that what we all should aspire to have? Can you dig it?

Twinkle, Twinkle, Little Star

When visiting my parents one Christmas holiday, I heard my three-year-old niece plunking away at the piano in their living room. As she banged her hands randomly over the keys, she sang a childhood lullaby that pays homage to the celestial wonders we see at night. Her voice was strong and confident: "Twinkle, twinkle little star. How I wonder what you are. Up above the world so high…" At the time, I was working as a personal assistant to a well-known actor in Los Angeles. I couldn't help but recognize the truth of these fabled lyrics. Her words echoed the thoughts of the modern-day celebrity enthusiast who is similarly captivated by the luster and allure of these romanticized star figures. Her words also carried a strong reminder that people and things aren't always what they appear to be.

People have always asked whether I would ever consider writing a tell-all book of my adventures in the entertainment field. They figure I must have interesting stories to share with the inquisitive public. After all, I have had the opportunity to work with a handful of noted film and television performers. Surely, there was intrigue, gossip, innuendo, indiscretions, and never-before-known secrets that only I could expose. My first response has always been, "Who cares?" And my second response has always been, "Who cares?"

I certainly don't. (And for the record, I do, in fact, possess bits of information only I will ever know and will carry with me 'til my final days on earth.) Having been close to the luster of these stellar beings, my advice to anyone is to keep a safe distance and continue to admire from afar. The closer you get, the more you lose sight of the wonder. The brilliance appears to have been an illusion. If you've ever studied the solar system or if you can even recall what you were taught in fourth grade science class, you know that a star is really a burning mass of illuminated gases. You can't catch a falling star, and you can't put it in your pocket. It's not possible. Similarly, you can't define or engage Hollywood stars with any confidence and put them in perspective. It's not possible.

But whether you're gazing from your own backyard or from the red carpet of a premiere, both of these heavenly and earthly diamonds are mysterious, intriguing, and captivating. We wonder how they got there. We wonder how long they'll last. We wonder whether they're closer to earth or closer to heaven. They make us wonder.

People, whether celebrities or not, aren't what they appear to be. Want to know people better? Travel with them. Dine with them. Work with them. The closer we inhabit someone's intimate space and personal environment, the more we learn and begin to know. And sometimes, we regrettably wish we had known less.

I'm not placing responsibility on the admired. I'm placing responsibility on the admirers. We (I said *we*) set expectations. We hold people in regard without really knowing them. We assume that the persona reflected by celebrities during a talk show interview or during a performance is the actual person we should have over for pot roast. And what about the everyday folks who populate our lives? Our friends, romantic partners, family, coworkers, and bosses? Same story, different galaxy. We automatically assume the new bosses that welcomed us so warmly the first day on the job should definitely be on this year's Christmas list. But what if these people are wanted by the FBI? What if they go home and abuse their spouses or children? Just what if they're not very nice? We then become disappointed and wonder what is wrong with the world and why everyone has gone crazy.

When I was in the ninth grade, the most beautiful girl in school was a senior named Leigh Lewis. She was a star athlete. She was a star student. She was a star—period. When the school year drew to a close, the most exciting event, besides graduation, was receiving annuals (i.e., yearbooks). An annual signing party had been scheduled in the high school gymnasium. On the night of the party, the first thing I did after thankfully receiving my yearbook was to immediately find Leigh Lewis' senior class photo. I had never seen anything like it. She was stunning. She was royalty. And even better, her majesty was also in attendance that very night at the annual signing party.

I wanted desperately to approach her and tell her I was her biggest fan. I just didn't know how to do it. The little voice inside said, "Keep your distance, and don't go near the light. Appreciate her from afar as you would any work of art." Instead, a bigger voice told my little voice to shut up and pipe down. Being a brave coward, I waited and made a weak attempt to compliment her as she was walking out the door. What else was I supposed to do? Because she was graduating, I thought I would never have another chance to let her know just how special I thought she was. I might never see her again! I somehow managed a verbal discharge of sounds and syllables—or so I thought. My weak attempt was either unheard or ignored because she didn't acknowledge me when I spoke. She couldn't be dismissive and cruel. She was too beautiful to behave in such a manner. Did I not speak loudly enough? Did she not hear me? Either way, I was crushed. I stood in silence as she walked away toward her future, and I was left standing with mine.

Had I left her alone, my memory would still be of a stunning beauty unlike anyone I had ever known. Now, the memory was tarnished, and I wish I had listened to my inner voice. I would have been better off wondering, but I was responsible for my fantasy's undoing. Not her. It was I who had set expectations. As a result, the difference between what I envisioned and what I experienced was light years apart.

I picked up my 1978 high school annual today and turned to the page with Leigh Lewis's senior photo. I no longer saw a star. The image of a beautiful blonde with a gorgeous summer tan had been replaced. Instead, I saw a fat little boy standing alone by the steps of the high school gymnasium.

No one asks to us to admire stars in the sky or people on the earth. No one asks us to adore, champion, exalt, or memorialize these stellar beings. We just do. We are struck and attracted by the beauty of things and people, and we want to be closer to touch, smell, and see. Just like the stars we see at night, the radiance of people and things are something to behold. And just like the childhood song we've heard so often, we wonder what they are.

Science implores us to delve into the unknown—to research, to experiment, and to explore. The hope is that we will discover something wondrous and that revelations will unfold. But sometimes, it's best to just keep wondering about our little stars.

Greater Than, Less Than

I never thought I would ever catch on to the "greater than" and "less than" arithmetic lessons Mrs. Ruby Smith taught in the second grade. I even had a hard time drawing the arrows. My arrow signs looked like disfigured beaks that belonged to genetically defective birds. I knew that five was larger than two, and I knew three was less than six. But, when I tried diagramming this mathematical fact with directional arrows, I simply lost all notion of numeric values as they related to one another. I have since mastered the sign language of arithmetic and understand perfectly the relationship between most sets of numbers.

However, when it comes to people, it's 1971 all over again, and I'm sitting in the front seat of the second row in Mrs. Smith's class, scratching my head. But this time around, numbers aren't involved in the equation. Now, I'm trying to understand the people who always tend to believe that everyone but themselves exists on the less-than side of the arrow sign with the disfigured beak.

I have a saying regarding one particular friend of mine: *her pain is greater than mine.* Regardless of what I say, mention, or reference, Toni exceeds me in every capacity. Her day was busier. Her boss was more neurotic. Her loss was greater. Her schedule more hectic. Her arm more broken (I exaggerate, of course). No matter what I begin to talk about, she interrupts with a sampling of her life that is simply "more" than mine. More busy, more important, more happy, more sad, more shocked, and more pained. More. More. More. Rarely does she take a breath. In fact, the few times she indulges me the chance to speak, I don't believe she's listening to me. I think she's figuring out what she's gonna say next. In her case, I don't feel as if it's a deliberate attempt to one-up me or anyone else. I think she is starved for attention and validation. As a result, every interface yields a conversation in which the scales tip in her favor. She needs to feel of greater value. She needs to be greater than.

Another acquaintance named Lorrie equally manipulates the scales toward greatness. While she doesn't talk as much as Toni, Lorrie's greater significance is derived from quality, not quantity. It's what she says, not how much she says. She asks me, "I hear you went to London? Where did you stay, and how long were you there?" The questions seem innocent enough. Nope. My answers simply provide a benchmark for comparison. Sure enough, this inquisitive and worldlier acquaintance has also been to London, several times, stayed at more luxurious hotels and stayed for longer and more meaningful amounts of time. Who knew that leisure travel would offer a playing field of competition? Again, on some level, a strong need for validation exists, and insecurity seems to account for this obnoxious habit.

Even when I was talking with Daddy one night, I happened to mention that I had gotten very little sleep the previous night and was therefore very tired. Guess what? He got less sleep and was more tired. I told him another time that I had pulled something in my back and had been suffering from a muscle strain. You guessed it. He too had recently been down in the back. I'll forgive Daddy, because he's my daddy. And nothing compares to knowing you're more like your daddy than not—

pain or no pain. But, for the rest of the "greater-thans," I've raised the white flag. I surrender. You are more special and deserving. You win.

As a result, I've become the quintessential bump-on-the-log. For example, if someone asks how my day is going, I simply reply, "Fine." If someone questions me and wants to know what exciting things I did over the weekend, I respond, "Not a thing." And, if someone recognizes me and wants to know what is new with me since we last saw each other twenty years ago, I answer, "Nothing." Although bland and uninspiring, my modus operandi is not without merit. With a minimal level of response and detail, I cut to the chase and allow inquiring minds to simply get on with the parade of superlatives that describe their grander and greater-than lives.

I save the most intimate and meaningful of thoughts and conversations for only a handful of people. With this select group of folks, no scales apply. No values are implied. No imbalance exists. We are not defined by greater than or less than. Instead, we only aspire to be better, not better than.

It seems as though inequality is inherent in our society. Is it just human nature? Since the beginning of time, the world has witnessed both nations and neighbors wage war over differences in religion, differences in notions of sovereignty, differences in skin color, and just plain differences. One side is different than the other. One side is greater than. I'm just curious, is it me, or has the concept of "greater than *or equal to*" never occurred to anyone else? I know the idea was taught in my third grade class. Just ask Mrs. Shirley Johnson. She ought to know. She was my third grade teacher. And she's my mama.

Toughskins

Thank goodness for the Sears catalog. From within its bound pages was my salvation—pants that fit, pants a fat boy could wear. The "husky" line of Toughskins pants offered comfort and hope—hope because I figured there was someone, somewhere who knew that little boys with big weight problems existed and were deserving. What I discovered after years of wearing the husky-size pants was that I had strengthened my character in so many ways. I had become resilient in withstanding any shame or embarrassment as a result of my size. I had also survived the torture and cruelty of other people. I had become the label I wore. I emerged from adolescence with a strong mind and even tougher skin.

Having been overweight as a child and through most of my teenage years, I can comment on being fat with a certain degree of expertise. There's no easy way through it or around it. Obesity is a challenge, but, for children and teens, weight issues are more overwhelming to manage. When you're an adult and suffer from obesity, you have a larger degree of awareness and knowledge regarding your situation. You are more conscious of cause and effect. You know what should be done, whether you decide to resolve the situation or not. And, adults typically have stronger problem-solving skills as well.

Obese adults certainly face their own challenges and issues. Self-doubt and low self-esteem are not respectful of age. Whether you're thirteen or thirty-three, these dark, emotional creatures viciously attack anyone who boasts an ounce of vulnerability. But for young minds and bodies that are still in development—still impressionable and still internalizing the world around them—obesity colors perceptions and has the potential for damaging, lifelong effects. For me, the effects of adolescent obesity have been lifelong but not damaging.

Managing to survive adolescence would have been much less difficult had I not had an extra thirty or so pounds to manage as well. My defense strategy for getting through embarrassing and humiliating moments, especially at school, was to watch the clock and wait for the bell. If someone was picking on me during a break, during recess, or between classes, I knew the bell would eventually ring and a classroom setting would soon offer a safer haven. I realized that every moment had its beginning and ending and that nothing, whether good or bad, lasts forever. Whatever I might have had to endure, it would not last any longer than a finite period of time.

Time would save me. Time would pass. The next period would come. The next day would come. The next week would come. The next semester would come. The next year would come. I would eventually get through anything with the passage of time because *nothing lasts forever.* Each time I survived a situation, I was more prepared the next time. And there was always a next time, so I waited.

I was never surprised or shocked when the next incident occurred. When I entered seventh grade and began junior high school, I realized very quickly that the innocence of elementary school was gone. Now, I was in the big leagues. Most of my former classmates from elementary school would be joining me as we moved to a new campus. I felt some comfort in knowing that I would not be alone in this new adventure. I was wrong. Within days of starting school, my best friend all through elementary school told me he was embarrassed to be seen with me because I was fat.

We had been friends since second grade. But now that we were teenagers, we were in a new school with lots of new faces, and we were facing the task of impressing those around us. I had become a liability. I had gained considerably more weight over the summer. At this point, I was fatter than I had ever been in my life. I understood perfectly. I said nothing and walked away. I gave him the space he needed.

PE (physical education) class was the most nightmarish ordeal during junior high school. This component of the school's curriculum provided the most opportunity for humiliation. How does a teenage boy who is thirty-pounds overweight tumble, flip, and balance through a gymnastics rotation? He doesn't. But the performance is a favorite among those in the audience. I was eternally grateful when I had to get braces for my teeth. The orthodontist gave me an excuse to sit out of class for three days. I was able to avoid the requirement of doing somersaults on the trampoline. My classmates were disappointed.

By my freshman year in high school, I was still affectionately known as, "Dean, Dean the Butterbean—Fattest Man I've Ever Seen," while I continued to grow larger. Despite the lengthy moniker and continued teasing, I felt a momentary sense of relief when I learned that a new policy had been introduced: all PE students would be required to wear uniforms. Maybe I would blend in with my other classmates. Maybe I would be lost in the sea of uniformity. The momentary relief was, in fact, short-lived as any hope of camouflaging my weight diminished the moment I stepped into the locker room. Three colors of uniforms were available—*according to size.* If you wore a small size, you received a blue T-shirt and blue shorts. If you wore a medium size, you received a red T-shirt and red shorts. And for the large size? Green. I knew I would be the sole green standout in my third period class. I couldn't do it. I wouldn't do it. I insisted on red. Because the clothes were so ill fitting and tight, I could barely run down the court or pass the ball during the basketball game moments later. The next day, I was St. Patrick incarnate and accepted the greenery.

If you're the modest type and think changing clothes in front of other people or perfect strangers is awkward, imagine what it's like when you're thirteen years old and extremely overweight. Changing clothes in front of forty other teenage boys whom you know is far worse. The others knew I didn't look like them. I knew I didn't look like the others, but they thought I needed reminding. And they reminded me almost every day. I had two choices: I could disrobe in front of my classmates and endure the teasing, or I could change clothes in a bathroom stall and be called a coward. I chose the teasing. In time, class would be over and fourth period would start. In time, the day would be over and another would start—in time, because *nothing lasts forever.*

There were many more hurtful instances that I endured during my heavy years. And there were many people who said many things to me every day. It's not important to detail or chronicle every instance or every comment. What's important to note is that I survived, and my Toughskins pants were with me every step of the way. Whatever I endured, I was simply thrilled to have pants that fit me—one of each color: brown, blue, red, and green. I would have been embarrassed beyond belief if my clothes had to have been made. Instead of being depressed, morose, sullen, reclusive, or fearful, I was simply glad to have clothes to wear, parents who supported me, and plenty of food to eat. That's right. I ate "good," and I enjoyed every mouthful. Despite what I went through at school each day, I was a happy person.

I'm even happier today because I found my way through those difficult years. It made me a strong person capable of enduring, accepting, and understanding. I became disciplined in the ability to withstand periods of conflict, uncertainty, fear, and pain. And finally, those years gave me the compassion to both sympathize and empathize with others who don't appear to fit in or those who fail to conform. Consequently, I try not to judge people for any type of superficial or aesthetic reason—for any reason. My condemnations and judgments are reserved for people who embrace ignorance through an inability to accept others' differences from their own perceived norms.

There are no invisible shields or coats of armor to protect the weak from the oppressive, but once the storms pass, there is much to be gained from having survived. Strength and strength of character emerge. I'm lucky and fortunate to have survived with a sense of resilience and with a newfound skin.

I was always happy to see Mama walk in the house with the newest Sears catalog. It meant that we might be ordering a new pair of husky Toughskins. And why not? They were certainly a good deal for the price. Neither of us had any idea of the mileage, wear, or value I'd get out of those pants.

The Need to Know

At the age of thirty-seven, I figured out one thing that I inherited from my daddy: the need to understand people, to know them without having any kind of relationship with them, to determine what motivates them to behave a certain way, and to somehow figure out why they do the things they do. By nature, Southerners have been known to be the *inquisitive* type. And by way of my DNA inheritance, an extra helping of this need for knowledge assured me that regardless of whether I was observing human behavior or just had a hankerin' to know the neighbor's business, I maintained an on-going *need to know*. Of course, this inquisitive mindset is obviously conditioned on the notion that we (Daddy and me) did and do everything normally, sanely, with good intent, or, better yet, the right way. I didn't realize how much like my daddy I was until I was driving home one evening from Blockbuster with my roommate. But now I know.

While in Blockbuster, I ran into an acquaintance that I had met previously through mutual friends. I had seen this person on several occasions, and we knew each other by name. When we passed each other in the store, he spoke to me as if we were in a funeral home or library. In turn, I acknowledged this confusing need for discretion with my own subtle nod and quiet "hello." The greeting was uneventful and without any noticeable enthusiasm. I felt like two allies in the enemy camp who were secretly exchanging glances. I, on the other hand, wanted to step up, slap him on the back, and say, "Hey, funny running into you on this side of town! What's new with you? It's good to see you!" I was enthusiastic about running into someone I knew in the most unexpected place. But, the greeting exchange was lifeless, almost clandestine. And I couldn't for the life of me figure out why he had behaved this way upon seeing me.

On the way home, I obsessed over the brief encounter. Finally, my roommate had heard enough. She said, "Would you get over it? Why do you go on and on about stuff the way you do?" I didn't verbalize an answer to her, but I knew the answer. I get it from my daddy. He's the same way. We just want to understand why people are the way they are. We just need to know.

As a child, our big event each week was "going to town." Because we lived on a farm, I always looked forward to the drive into the local town each Saturday. To a little boy, Conway, South Carolina, offered the city life and civilization—a grocery store, a mall, and a McDonald's. While at the mall, Daddy would usually sit outside on a bench until Mama, my brother, and I finished shopping or browsing in the stores. Sometimes, I would sit with him and just watch people as they came and went.

Daddy studied each person as if they were under a microscope. He had comments on practically everybody that walked by. He couldn't figure out why some particular woman was with the man she was with—especially because this man was known to "ride the roads" (a subtle reference used in the South, which basically means carousing) and run around with other women. Daddy couldn't understand why another woman would let her children run around like hellions without supervision. I was always warned that my brother and I better not think about such bad behavior. And, he always reminded me that if his daddy had ever caught him behaving like that, a switch would have made multiple contacts with his backside. Duly noted.

To make matters worse, he couldn't understand why a lady in the parking lot was taking so long to get in her car, put the key in the ignition, and back out so someone else could park in her space. He would sit there and start grinding his teeth, while the woman in the parked car obviously fished through her purse, looked in the pocket of the car, and looked through her shopping bags. He had no patience. He always wanted to know, "Why in the hell can't she wait to get home to go through all that mess!" I had to agree, and it became natural for me to simply question why people do the things they do.

One summer evening, Daddy took my brother and me to one of his clubhouse fish dinners. The clubhouse, owned by a friend of Daddy's, was a cabin-like dwelling built on the edge of a lake near the Little Pee Dee River. It was set deep in the woods in a remote rural area and was surrounded by pine trees as far as the eyes could see. It always seemed to be the kind of place where movies about swamp creatures might be made. This clubhouse certainly didn't sport a tennis court, golf course, or swimming pool. It was simply a small cement blockhouse where the menfolk gathered to cook fish, commune, and get away from their wives.

On this occasion, Daddy cooked supper for everybody. There were around ten of his friends plus my brother and me. He made a big pot of fish stew and a big pot of white rice. Homemade sweet pickles and a loaf of white bread completed the meal. One of Daddy's friends ate two heaping plates of the fish stew and rice. After he had finished the second serving, he smacked his lips and then said to Daddy, "Bobby, that stew was just a touch too salty." I could hardly believe my ears. Especially since I had sat right by him and watched as the broth from the stew ran down the corner of his mouth with almost every bite. He would catch each drop and dribble with his tongue like it was the last drop and dribble of stew left in the pot. As a five-year-old, I felt sorry for Daddy. As an adult, I am annoyed by the comment his friend made. What was he thinking?

He had just eaten two plates of stew and rice, and he had the nerve to comment that the stew was not to his liking? Go figure some people. If that stew had been the worst thing I ever tasted, I would have never even thought to tell the cook that his work was less than anything but perfect. It wasn't good manners, and it wasn't nice—period. So the question remained, why would somebody say something like that?

Of course, I still can't figure out the nerve of some people. I've been to gatherings and parties where everyone brings some potluck item. For example, somebody may be asked to bring a dip, a salad, chips, or a dessert. Whatever the item, my belief is that the item is prepared and brought for others to enjoy. If the item somehow doesn't get eaten, I've always insisted the host keep it as a token of appreciation for having hosted the party. "No, please keep the dip and enjoy it this week. I had such a great time," or, "Just toss those uneaten chips. I don't need or want them. Do you?"

But I've watched some people scrape the remaining dip, even if it's a tablespoon's worth, place it in a to-go container, and head out the door. I've watched people clandestinely make a take-home plate filled with everything offered at the party, just to have for later. And I've seen people pour crumbs from the bowl back into the empty potato chip bag. As God is my witness, you'll never see me resort to such desperate and pathetic behavior. Why would people do such things? Are potato chip crumbs really appetizing? Are they in danger of becoming extinct? Does the cat prefer a leftover holiday dip to Tender Vittles? Does walking out the door with remnants of your party platter alert the other guests to your initial contribution? Are people so cheap they would rather focus on securing the next round of provisions through social etiquette violations (i.e., taking food from buffet bars when you ordered from the menu) than care what someone thinks of them? Are these people (who we thought we knew but really don't) so normal after all? Why? Why? Why?

I suppose there will never be an answer to why people take their pot-luck contributions back home. There may never be an answer to why people spend an eternity holding a parking spot while somebody else waits. Bad manners will never be explained, regardless of how tasteful the meal is. People will always respond differently to you depending on where you see them. There simply will never be an answer to the questions we ask ourselves about someone else's behavior.

I have tried to learn acceptance, to simply let people and things be, but regardless of the passive disposition I try to adopt, it never quells my need to know. I get that from my daddy.

World's Finest

When I was leaving a friend's home late one afternoon, I was surprised by a comment he made as I got in my car. Upon saying good-bye, he added, "I could go for a good candy bar."

I was struck by this last intonement, because my friend, Steven, never expresses any specific wish, need, desire, want, or taste for any particular food. He eats when he's hungry. His diet is as simple as are his dining experiences. He eats methodically and without haste. Eating is a mere necessity for him and not an indulgence or means of enjoyment. He has never expressed an affinity for any particular dish, cuisine, flavor, or restaurant. As a result, there is no fanfare over his culinary tastes. His meals come and go without notice. But this evening, out of nowhere, came an atypical request for a good candy bar.

On the way home, I pondered this curious statement and could find no reason as to why he had suddenly found a sweet tooth along with the need to verbalize it. But, his comment did prompt me to conclude that times ain't what they used to be. People, and the world we live in, have changed.

The most delicious candy bars I've ever had in my life are the ones I used to buy from schoolmates who were usually trying to raise money for new band uniforms, a trip to the state fair, or new cheerleading pom-poms. The candy bar? World's Finest. It was wrapped in the most beautiful silver foil that was additionally encased in a lovely white wrapper. The words *World's Finest* were boldly imprinted on this white, sleek wrapper, and never had truer words been written or spoken. It was the finest candy bar in the world and the best I have ever tasted in my life.

The milk chocolate was smooth. The toasted almonds, evenly distributed throughout the bar with precision skill, provided just the perfect salt fix to counter the sugar factor. While the bar was conveniently designed to be shared (it was divided into sections that could be easily broken off), there was no way anybody was having even one taste of my World's Finest.

The cost of the candy bar was exactly one dollar. Or, if you were economically challenged as many kids growing up in a rural farm community might be, you could also purchase half of the candy bar for fifty cents.

Looking back, I can't believe I actually purchased half of a candy bar from someone—not only because of sanitary reasons, but because I always seemed to buy the second half. Someone always beat me to the punch and purchased the first half. I was never so lucky as to be the one to get dibs on the initial break. Even more discouraging, the second half always seemed to look as if somebody's dog had gnawed on it like a bone. The foil was brutally mangled, and the white wrapper was viciously torn and shredded, with chocolate smudge spots appearing generously. God only knew what those second-half bars had been through before landing in my thankful hands. And the Lord only knows where they had been.

But I didn't care. I didn't care whether the band got new uniforms, whether the cheerleaders got new pom-poms, or whether the home economics department raised enough money to attend the state fair. I had my hands on the World's Finest candy bar.

These days, it's still not uncommon to see the candy bar as the cornerstone of fundraising endeavors. Some kids approached me one day in a mall parking lot in Los Angeles attempting to sell candy to raise money for their school. When I looked in their cardboard box, I saw the World's Finest delicacy mixed in with other name-brand confectionary delights. There they lay, the beautiful white wrappers covering the shiny foil, but I had no intention of purchasing candy from some stranger in a parking lot in Los Angeles.

Now, if it had been 1976, and I had been riding in a rickety old bus on a dirt road in South Carolina, I would have jumped at the chance to buy a dirty, battered second-half bar from Vickie Jane Todd. She would get to go to the state fair, and I would devour the sweetest morsel I had ever known for a grand total of fifty cents. But there was no way I would consider helping a questionably credible kid to support his worthy cause in the year 2002. Even if the bar was a full purchase and the wrapper was intact.

The notion of a candy bar prompted me to realize that the level of trust, honesty, simplicity, and innocence that I once assumed is now suspect in every word, gesture, action, or deed I encounter. And, it's not just me. It's everybody. I wish we all could return to the time when you could buy half of a candy bar with smudge marks on the wrapper without sensing distrust or danger. The world truly would be finer. But times ain't what they used to be. People, and the world we live in, have changed.

Easy as Pie (and Ham)

It doesn't matter what kind of dessert Mama serves with a meal. Be it cake or pie or some kind of puddin', Daddy adds his own unique finishing touch to the dessert du jour. And why? For the sake of finding a balance between the extremes of sweet and salty. You see, he requires a piece of salty meat, leftover from the main course, to minimize the dessert's high-level sweet factor. Whether it's a chicken wing, slice of ham, piece of fat back, chunk of roast, or sliver of sirloin, he counters the chocolate pie, coconut cake, or banana puddin' rather scientif-ically: he adds a piece of salty meat. While this may seem con-trary and incongruent from a strictly culinary standpoint, without fail he'll say to Mama, "Hand me a piece of that ham to go with this pie. I like a piece of meat to go with all this sweet." For him, this minor adjustment to the dinnertime finale appears to not only enhance the flavor and appeal, but ensures a balance. And, after all these years of watching him indulge his sweet tooth fancy in this atypical fashion, there appears to be a method to his madness. Perhaps his post-main course ritual goes so far as to offer a hopeful secret for finding life's elusive balance. At the very least, his mealtime fancy offers a figurative way of restating what we already knew: according to Robert B. "Bobby" Johnson, the middle ground between two extremes can be manipulated much like his adjustment and modification of the dessert plate. Too much sugar necessitates more salt. One extreme's effect is lessened with the inclusion of another extreme. If only life were that easy. And maybe it is as easy as pie—and ham.

Striking a balance in one's life has become an endless pursuit for most people. Although my Daddy can certainly understand the palatable leveling of salt and sugar, as far as taste goes, I can only imagine the confused look or reaction I would get if I asked him whether his life was balanced. His generation did not engage in such pursuits. They took the good with the bad. Feast came as did famine, and little thought was given to the internal search for some feeling of contentment or equilibrium.

As a child, my only recollection of anything remotely related to the much coveted state of balance was in relation to its exact opposite. In this polar opposite condition, all sense and sensibility collapsed and the soul was lost in ruin. This condition held mystique, invoked fear, and seldom offered a guarantee of recovery. The mere mention of the words would send chills down my spine. This condition had a name: *nervous breakdown*. I can still hear Mama saying, "They've taken so-and-so to Columbia. I heard it was a nervous breakdown." Columbia, South Carolina, was home of the state mental hospital and was located on Bull Street. Any reference or mention of Bull Street conjured images and notions of the insane and maladjusted.

It was hard to imagine how a mental breakdown actually occurred. Did people fall to the floor quivering and shaking? Did they speak in unintelligible terms? Were they carried off in straitjackets while crying and screaming? I found the whole concept unsettling because there never seemed to be answers to my questions. No one had ever seen a nervous breakdown. No one knew what a nervous breakdown may look like, sound like, or behave like. Every nervous breakdown was uniquely different. And for sure, no one had evidence of a cure. I only knew one person who experienced a nervous breakdown. This lady will remain unnamed for the sake of her privacy and integrity. I can say that she was not the same person after the breakdown as she was before. She even looked differently. Something in her eyes spoke of loss. There was a faraway stare that seemed to search for hope and resolution. And, when I had the opportunity to see her face-to-face for the first time upon her release from the hospital, I instinctively knew that hope and resolution would not be among her discoveries any-time soon—or ever.

After that day, the concept of a nervous breakdown no longer induced fear. Instead, I felt sadness—as seen through the eyes of this woman I knew. I envisioned her sense of loss and hopelessness. I felt her need to find resolution. I wished for her return to a state of balance. *Balance.* A common ground of two extremes.

Today, society is driven to find a mental compass that reflects an evenly distributed directional pattern. Gurus, life healers, spiritual coaches, self-help books, seminars, exercise, sabbaticals, and the like are employed, engaged, and consumed in that endless search for individual resolution on a higher mental plane. I've desired and sought this well-touted state of being myself. If just one of the aforementioned resources can restore the mental state of calm and peace that we all so desperately desire and need, then let the pursuit begin. I don't think I ever want to look into someone's eyes again and see hopelessness and despair. Life is too wonderful and far too short for imbalance to exist for too long, if at all.

However, should all else fail, think about my daddy's simple formula. In other words, I'd suggest a piece of ham with your next serving of pie. I can testify that the unique balance of salt and sweet have seemed to serve him pretty well. Maybe he's on to something. Life may just be as easy as pie—and ham.

Fear Not.
God Is Great, God Is Good.

I was raised to say the blessin' and give thanks before each meal. I was taught right from wrong. I knew most of the words to the gospel hymns such as "Amazing Grace" and "What a Friend We Have in Jesus." Up until the time I started college, Mama took my brother and me to church practically every Sunday. We attended revivals, and we attended Vacation Bible School. I've heard people speak in tongues as the Holy Spirit filled their souls, and I've seen people baptized in the Little Pee Dee River.

If I were building a resume for heaven, perhaps these religious indulgences, which were heavily influenced by Southern Baptist doctrines, would secure my admission through and beyond the Pearly Gates. My true sense of spirituality, however, evolved outside the doors of the little Baptist church I attended as a child. Just like a child's mealtime prayer, I do believe that God is great and that God is good. I also believe He's everywhere. You just can't be afraid to go lookin' for him, or be fearful of finding him, either.

My first recollection of church, religion, or organized faith was sitting in the choir section of a small Southern Baptist church and watching my mama play the piano while the congregation and choir sang along. When the song was over, she would get up from the piano and come sit by me on the front pew in the choir section until it was time for another song. Then one day, she wasn't playing the piano anymore. All of a sudden we were sitting with the rest of the congregation. It was years later when I learned exactly why she was no longer needed as the church pianist: *she was a Methodist.*

Talking about the difference between Baptists and Methodists is like talking about the difference between fried chicken and baked chicken. It's the preparation that differentiates the two. There's nothing wrong with either. They're just two different tastes of the same food. I didn't belong to either church affiliation. I simply attended the Baptist church located within our farm community because it was five minutes down the road from our house.

Mama belonged to the Methodist church in Aynor, South Carolina, where she was born and raised. When she married Daddy and moved out to the country, I assume it made sense for her to take my brother and me to the Baptist church near our house. Because it was geographically closer? Because it offered more spiritual enlightenment? Probably not. Since Mama taught school in the community and Daddy was a farmer in the community, I suppose it just seemed natural for us to participate in the community church. So Mama stopped attending her home church in Aynor altogether. Although she never joined the Baptist church, she did attend as if she were a member. For the official record, her Methodist affiliation and membership remained with her hometown church. However, her faith was universal and steadfast, regardless of the location or denomination.

Because she could play the piano and because there wasn't a regular church member available who could play the piano, she gladly helped out when the leaders of the Baptist church called upon her to serve as the pianist. I think she enjoyed playing for the congregation and participating in the Sunday service. But one day, someone joined the church that did play the piano, and Mama was no longer needed. She was thereby dismissed. I think she understood the need to have the pianist be a member of the church, but the diplomacy and tact with which the dismissal was handled left much to be desired. I'm not sure this incident helps explain any theological or technical differences among Baptists, Methodists, or any other affiliation. It simply helps to understand that the differences are significant and that they matter a great deal.

The Baptist church we attended maintained a membership of maybe one hundred or so "God-fearin' brothers and sisters." They were all brothers and sisters in Christ's name. This qualifier was used in addressing each other not only during the church services but also during daily conversations: "Brother Henry, would you lead us in prayer?" and "Sister Linda, that was a mighty fine mess of collards you took over to Sister Mary's. I know she appreciates you doin' that." The members of this church were all good people whose intention was to worship and celebrate the love of Jesus Christ as any God-fearin' Christians should. What I neither understood nor agreed with was the *fearin'* part. To me, reverence toward God should have been described with more joyous, uplifting, and compassionate terms—not by using the word *fear* or by utilizing fear.

When I was in junior high school, a classmate I had known came to school one day a completely different person. Timmy had been to a church revival service the previous evening and had been saved. He had committed his life to serving the Lord because he was so afraid. After hearing the preacher's sermon, Timmy said that he would have ended up with the devil if he hadn't come forward and confessed his sins. As is customary in a Southern Baptist church, when the sermon is finished, the preacher implores, even begs, members of the congregation who are sinners and who have not been saved to publicly come forward, kneel before the altar, and ask God into their hearts. (In a Methodist church, the preacher "invites" or "asks" the sinners to come forward. Another difference between the two styles.)

And that's just what my friend had done the night before. He had come forward, shaking in his shoes. I asked him if he understood what he had done. My question was to determine whether he realized the nature of his commitment. I didn't doubt the legitimacy of what he had done. I was truly impressed by his bravery, and I just wanted to know whether he comprehended the magnitude of this responsibility. He said, "Well, it's better to be scared out of hell than to burn in it." I understood from that point how fear was instrumental. I just didn't agree with the tactic. I didn't agree with a lot of tactics. I agreed with the common goal everyone wished to achieve, but I found myself challenging the process. There were plenty of reasons to challenge the process.

I once participated in a field trip with my Sunday school class. I was terribly excited to be going on an all-day excursion where I would get to ride in van that had been rented from the local Chevrolet dealer. What a way to spend a Saturday when you're eleven years old! Plus, Mama had fried chicken for me to take as my lunch, and she had also put extra snacks in my lunch bag. I was excited to be going on a trip or anywhere for that matter. So my teacher and the handful of Sunday school class members, including myself, headed out for a day of adventure and fellowship.

Our Sunday school teacher was not only new to the position, she was a relatively new member of the church. What does a church do with a new member? Get them involved—

even though neither she nor very many of my Sunday school teachers had instructional training with regard to classroom education. Volunteerism is imperative in small, rural churches, and repentance is usually enough qualification to instill God's wisdom into impressionable minds. With this teaching assignment, I often wondered whether she was comfortable with the new responsibility. If she was or wasn't, she had won my admiration and support for having arranged this trip. We piled into the van, and off we went.

The day ended when we stopped and ventured into a small gift shop, looking for souvenirs to take home. I had been given five dollars to spend. I was browsing in a corner at the back of the shop when my Sunday school teacher approached me. She asked, "Does your daddy still talk ugly?" I was speechless. There was no time for any thoughts of anger, surprise, disappointment, or betrayal—only fear.

Most everyone in the community was aware that my daddy didn't attend church regularly. And, I guess most knew that, in his day-to-day conversations with people, he was known to issue a swearword or two. But, my daddy was and is a good man. A great man. He used to fry fish for elderly people in the community who might not be feeling well enough to fix their own meals. He wanted to know they had something to eat. He would also help elderly widows who may have something around the house needing to be fixed. He visited people who were sick in the hospital or at home and made himself available to them, should they need anything at all. He gave of himself as much as anybody I know, and on this day, when I was having fun and trying to belong, my teacher embarrassed Daddy and me. I just knew that we were going to end up in the bad place. The secret couldn't be hidden any longer: Bobby

Johnson talked ugly sometimes. And who knows? Maybe his children did too. When she asked me if my daddy still talked ugly, I said, "No. But sometimes he still says *damn*."

I thought I had recovered pretty well. It was the best I could do, considering I was ill-prepared for the inquisition. In hindsight, I'm sure I only made matters worse. I did, however, make note of the fear factor once again, because one thing is for sure—I was scared.

When I was seven years old, my family and I spent one Sunday afternoon visiting these particular relatives who happened to be *big* (i.e., heavily involved) in their local church. Both parents of this family held notable positions within the ranks of church leadership and stewardship. Their children were active in the youth programs as well. They were the quintessential church family. During the visit to their home on this particular Sunday afternoon, I loudly exclaimed the words, "My Lord," while playing outside with one of the cousins. My exclamation was not intended as any type of obscenity. I probably said something as innocent as, "My Lord, the mosquitoes are bad out here," or, "My Lord, I'm tired of playing catch." My cousin proceeded to scold me because I had taken the Lord's name in vain, thus breaking one of the Ten Commandments.

I tried to explain it was just a figure of speech and that no harm was meant. After all, hadn't everybody said "My Lord" before? He then went and summoned his mother who also lectured me on taking the Lord's name in vain. By the time I left their house that Sunday, I was dead sure I was headed even further south, where the temperature gets real, real hot. I left their home feeling unworthy and ashamed. And frightened.

A few years later, one of the deacons in our church decided he wanted to preach the word of God. He attended a local seminary school and was later ordained as a preacher with the right to "have" a church of his own. I thought members of the church would have supported this news, but they didn't. Instead, the news seemed to fuel jealousy and contempt in some members of the congregation. Maybe they were threatened. Maybe they were jealous.

Regardless of the reasons, this man's decision to begin preaching created factions within the congregation. Matters were made worse when he was asked to preach one Sunday at our church—the very church he had always attended. Some saw it as a celebration of his newfound role and thought the opportunity would recognize his accomplishment. Others felt it was an act of showmanship. Or maybe someone thought he was attempting to fill the vacancy in our church, since we had no full-time preacher at the time. I never understood the source of discontent since this man was both eager and willing to preach God's word. I wondered what the big deal was, because God's love was based on the premise of loving one another. What did it matter who was doing it, as long as it was being done?

On the Sunday he preached, a dinner was planned immediately following the service and was served in the fellowship hall. When everyone assembled for dinner, they found a package sitting on a table. The package was intended for the newly ordained preacher. He opened it. Inside were the extracted parts from a farm animal. No one ever admitted to being responsible for the vulgar act, nor was it ever confirmed who sent the surprise package. I'm not sure whether a card with any kind of greeting was left with the package, but fear and intimidation were certainly part of the message.

Our church went without a preacher for a long while, but, eventually, someone was hired that met with everyone's approval. Much to my surprise, this new pastor was actually a distant relative of Daddy. He and Daddy knew each other. Naturally, we made it a point to invite the new preacher, his wife, and their daughter to our house for Sunday dinner. I'm sure members of the congregation were happy that he was coming to our house. Maybe there was hope for us after all! Maybe he could work his magic and convert us into full-fledged members of the church! I have to admit I was nervous about him coming for dinner. I thought we would have to "put on the dog" just to try and impress him. I didn't want him to think we were hopelessly destined for a less-than-comfortable afterlife.

But my worries were soon assuaged. As soon as I saw what Mama was serving for dinner, I knew this preacher couldn't care less who the devil tempted that day. She had made country-fried steak, shrimp casserole, macaroni and cheese casserole, peas, rice and gravy, homemade biscuits, and sweet potato soufflé. Sitting at the table, I knew this meal was enough redemption to save us from the fires of damnation. The meal was fine, everyone was happy, and there was no real pressure to convert us sinners. For once, I wasn't scared. I felt at peace.

It's only been in the last few years of my life that I have found my own peace with the God I know and trust. The most profound statement I ever heard came from a friend one night while we were sitting in a bar, of all places, having margaritas. She said, "If you know God, you walk in love." Her statement left an indelible impression on me.

I thought back to the times in my life when so many others had tried to share their understanding of God with me. I suspect many of these people did not truly walk in love; they walked in fear. It's all they had ever known. Intimidation and humiliation were means to knowing the Lord. I appreciate their intent. I disagree with the tactics. I'm not saying it's an easy task to help guide people along the path to spiritual enlightenment. Most people need help with the journey. Others don't. And still, some may never come to know this place. But if there is a journey, fear should be left behind, or nothing will ever be ventured or gained.

As much as I saw, heard, and experienced during my earlier days in the little Baptist church in our community, I always knew that there was more to God than a judgment system based on whether you were Baptist or Methodist, whether your daddy talked ugly, whether you took the Lord's name in vain, or whether you served fried steak or fried chicken to the preacher. I always felt there was a grander, more unconditional love that God wanted us to know.

I think religion and spirituality are as unique to human beings as their fingerprints. As such, people should go about the business of worshipping a God, trusting in the universe, or walking in love the way that best nourishes their souls. I'm glad I was patient enough to allow my own inclinations to develop. I should thank the members of the little Baptist church for indirectly helping me to find my way in the spiritual world. I did learn from them that God is great and that He is good. But, what I learned on my own was that we must each define what God means to us as individuals. I also learned that finding God or embracing any type of spiritual lifestyle should be liberating and free—and more than anything, free from fear.

Southern Comfort

The way to a man's heart is through his stomach. As society becomes more and more conscious of political correctness, I assume "a man's heart" implies mankind in general—men and women, or anyone's heart that needs the comfort and warmth of a good meal, and not necessarily for the intent of romantic or amorous pursuit. Good food has a way of alleviating hurt, pain, and mental discomfort. In the South, there's nothing like a buffet of fried chicken, macaroni and cheese, chicken bog, country ham, biscuits, potato salad, cream-style corn, deviled eggs, chocolate cake, and every food imaginable to help ease the pain of losing a loved one. The hospitality of dying has never been so good.

There is great skill in the art of expressing kindness, compassion, and consolation, especially during times when tragedy, loss, and shock abound. Eloquence should define the moment. Heartfelt words and gestures are necessary, needed, and welcomed. And because the South carries the reputation for having cornered the market on hospitality, most people would assume heartache and its villainous nature are assuaged with a sweet drawl and gentle nature. But not completely. It takes both a homemade coconut cake and kind words to best convey thoughts of sympathy.

When my paternal grandmother, Tronie Johnson, died, I was only ten years old. I had never been exposed to the concept of loss. I had experienced the loss of pets but never people. My grief in learning she had passed away was grief for my daddy, mostly. He was the baby of his family and had been the one sibling who remained on the homestead to farm the land and look after his mama. We had lived the length of a football field from Grandma Tronie with nothing but plowed dirt between the houses. We could clearly see each other's property and knew pretty much what was happening within the other's household on a daily basis. Daddy and Grandma Tronie shared a very special, loving, devoted, comfortable, and familiar relationship. They were close and similarly lived close to each other. Rarely a single day went by that they didn't see each other. He took great care of her.

A couple of years before she actually died, she was hospitalized with heart-related problems. I was sure she was going to die then, but she got better. On the day the doctor told our family she would be released from the hospital, Daddy became a new person. As we were walking out of the hospital, he stopped in front of an old oak tree, which looked to be a hundred years old. He spoke to the tree as if it was a person. He remarked how strong it looked and how long it had survived, and then he grabbed the tree and hugged it. I figured everything was going to be all right, and I realized how much Grandma Tronie meant to him.

My own relationship with Grandma Tronie was also very special. Since Daddy farmed and Mama taught school, she helped look after my brother and me when we were very young. If Grandma Tronie never did anything else for me, she introduced me to the Cold Plate special served at Nye's Drugstore. The chilled plate included a heaping of fresh chicken salad made with the sweetest mayonnaise I ever tasted, two slices of cheddar cheese, and two packs of Captain Wafer's crackers. Fresh lettuce and tomato were served as a garnish. It was a summertime dream.

My brother and I would sit in the wooden booth in our shorts and bare feet, devouring every bite. The plates were licked clean. Even though she was quite special to me, my own loss wasn't comparable to Daddy's loss. I understood whose pain was deservedly greater.

While the logistics of visitation and the ensuing funeral and graveside burial services were all new but easy to comprehend, I never got over the amount of food brought to Grandma Tronie's house by friends and neighbors. Every table was full. Every kitchen counter was full. Every sideboard was full. Bowls, platters, casserole dishes, and serving trays were visible everywhere you looked, and their respective contents were characteristically of Southern descent. I wasn't a stranger to country cookin' and good food. If you took one look at me, you could tell that I had never been denied table privileges; however, the degree to which food was available on this occasion was unlike anything I had ever seen. A sampling of the menu bears repeating: ham biscuits, butter beans, string beans, field peas, pots of neck bone and rice, salt-cured hams, platters upon platters of fried chicken, roast beef, stew beef, macaroni and cheese, potato salad, pear salad, pecan pies, red velvet cakes, chocolate cakes, and coconut cakes. And the provisions continued from the time the family was notified of the death until two days later, when she was laid to rest.

Grandma Tronie had a big family, which included seven sons, one daughter, seven daughters-in-law, a son-in-law, nieces, nephews, lots of grandchildren, and many friends. We all had big appetites, and we ate big. The only member of the family who refused to eat and whose despair seemed to be inconsolable was our bulldog, Nubbin. For two days, he lay in a hole dug out in the field beside Grandma's house and didn't come around for a single scrap. Nubbin had been accustomed to walking up to Grandma Tronie's every day where she would feed him handouts from the backporch steps. Somehow, he sensed she was gone.

It may seem perfectly understandable to the novice Southerner that such a voluminous amount of food was necessary because so many mouths needed to be fed, but the underlying gesture was far more significant. Family, friends, members of the community, and the local churchgoers knew that we needed to eat and to be "looked after," to be comforted in the most giving and generous of ways. And those ways meant preparing food. A family who is suffering the loss of a loved one is in no more a frame of mind to prepare food or keep the kitchen organized than a bride is to cook food and clean the church for her own wedding. It's just not done.

The excessive food was a sentiment of excessive sympathy. Every pot, dish, breadbasket, serving platter, and stainless-steel pot was filled with sympathetic condolence. Love and support was the primary ingredient within each of the baked, fried, and roasted offerings. Food was and is the way we care for each other. Making a meal and taking it to someone in need was a way of saying, "I understand, and I'm sorry." Expression without words is often the most heartfelt and understood.

As I grew older, other relatives died. My Grandma Dawsey (maternal grandmother), in addition to several aunts and uncles, eventually passed away. The sadness and emptiness of loss never changed. Nor did the ritual and routines of caring for the bereaved. The procession of sympathizers and the delivery of abundance began. And no matter how emotionally devastated someone might be, there was a moment of relief and comfort in the homemade servings of sympathy and tenderness.

Years later, when I was living away from home, a very close friend suffered the tragedy of loss for the first time when someone close to her died suddenly and tragically. My upbringing kicked into gear. There would be time for words of comfort much later. There would be time, later on, to console—to talk if she needed. I headed for the kitchen and began the process of helping her heal. I cooked. I prepared a feast. I made something to let her know that I would help share in her despair. And there's nothing like a good casserole to say, "In time, you'll heal. But in the meantime, this will make you feel somewhat better."

Everybody has a unique way of communicating. There are nations which speak languages exclusive to their own inhabitants. Cultures reflect traditions that define their domain. The South isn't without its own style of verbal and nonverbal discourse. There's nothing more characteristic than a lazy accent of thoughtful words, unless it's a lazy accent of thoughtful words served with a heap of good country cookin'. The comfort of living and dying in the South has never been better.

The Better Policy

Honesty is good, but not in all instances. I'm just saying it's not always the best policy, especially if you live in the South and somebody thinks you're "gettin' too big for your britches" or "gettin' above your raisins" (i.e., when someone thinks your ego is inflated or thinks you act high-and-mighty, considering how you were raised). Southerners are gonna let you know without beatin' around the bush. The intention is to impart some helpful advice that is honest—constructive criticism, if you will. I didn't say the observation was necessary, requested, desired, or even true. Just honest. But the refreshing candor of my fellow Southerners could stand a little tempering. There are times when honesty could take a back seat to the kinder and gentler acts of discretion and diplomacy. Without beatin' around the bush, let me just say that honesty ain't always the best policy. It's a good policy and most times a great policy. But there are better ones, sometimes.

One summer, while visiting my parents, I also took the time to spend an afternoon with my Aunt Doe. With her health failing and mind deteriorating, I felt the need to see her because I didn't know when I would be back in South Carolina. More importantly, I didn't know how much longer she would be alive. I shall preface this little story by saying I have changed in many ways over the years. I look differently. I dress differently.

Perhaps I've lost some of my accent. Maybe I don't eat as many fried foods as I once did. It's called evolving. Aunt Doe would have called it "puttin' on airs."

I drove out to her house with my brother and Daddy. When we arrived, Aunt Doe was sitting underneath her carport enjoying the summer afternoon breeze. Joining her were a home health nurse, her son and daughter-in-law, and a neighbor. I saw her smile as we pulled into the driveway. I smiled. I was glad to see her, and I was immediately glad I had decided to come home for a visit.

The moment I walked up, she took one look at me and said, "My Lord have mercy, the wind couldn't blow through your hair with all that mess in it." Allow me to explain. My hair was spiked and styled with a very dense hair product. OK, so it was a lot of hair pomade. Hey, it's not a crime. Who says I have to keep a bowl cut with bangs until I'm seventy-three? With her welcome-home message, I was relieved to know that some aspects of her well-being were functioning just fine. Her honesty was as healthy as a horse.

I wondered, at length, why she found it necessary to express this opinion in front of everyone who was visiting at the time I stopped by the house. Her honesty could have been saved for a quiet moment when we were alone together. Or better yet, she could have said, "Well look at you! You've changed so much. Every time I see you, something looks different." Her point could have easily been made with a less-direct expletive. I would have understood the point just the same. But Southern honesty doesn't always invite discretion to the dinner table. She didn't like my hair and thought I should know immediately. Honesty.

As a child growing up, it was always a thrill to spend each Saturday in the nearby town of Conway. We lived on a farm, and the weekend ritual of going to town meant exposure to a dime store (e.g., Woolworth's), restaurants (e.g., Burger Chef), and anything else that wasn't a pasture, a plow, or a fishing pond. It was something we looked forward to each week. On one particular Saturday afternoon, I was with Mama in the Jerry Cox Company (a local department store) when we happened to run into a former neighbor who used to live up the road from our house. It had been several years since I had seen this young woman as she had married and moved away from the community. Not much had changed since I last saw her except I was a few years older and a few pounds heavier. Mama reminded her who I was.

The woman replied that she could hardly believe I was now thirteen years old. Mama then commented, "Yes, he sure is growing up." The former neighbor responded, "Well, he's growing out for sure." She gestured with her arms and demonstrated the visual of a growing stomach. Obviously, I was still as fat as she remembered. She even laughed about it. There must be at least a thousand and one things she could have said rather than commenting on my growing belly. Here's one: "Well, you may be thirteen, but you haven't changed a bit!" Note to self: I'm still fat. Honesty.

On another visit home to spend time with my parents, I brought my Pilates videotape so I could continue with the new fitness and exercise regimen I had started back in Los Angeles. For anyone who is unfamiliar with this form of exercise, Pilates is a unique method of strengthening the entire body by focusing on the muscles of the abdominals and back. The process requires strict breathing patterns as well as strict attention to form and technique. I was in my bedroom performing the exercises when Daddy came walking by the door. He saw me stretched out on the floor and heard me inhaling and exhaling. His comment? "You're in a cult." I wasn't asked what I was doing or whether this was something beneficial to my health. I was now in a cult. Honesty.

I suppose my hair greatly interests people because Mama also found an opportunity one time to be as honest as Aunt Doe had been some years earlier. It actually happened during the same visit in which I was denounced a cult member. The preface to this hair story is that, as I have aged, I have tended to cover my receding hairline and thinning crown by employing a range of headwear. Baseball caps and ski caps (we call them *boggins*—slang for toboggan) are both in my wardrobe. I find it convenient to have one on hand when you wake up in the morning with pillow hair—especially if company shows up unexpectedly. And on this visit home, some high school classmates decided to stop by and say hello to our family. I had been awake for only a little while, so I grabbed a ski cap to put on my head. I realize I wasn't standing in the middle of a snowstorm and that it was not necessarily cold in the house. It was a hat to cover up an unkempt look, so forgive my vanity. The moment I walked into the den to greet our guests, Mama said, "He's got on that old boggin' cause he don't like to walk around the house without a hat unless his hair is fixed." No, she didn't. Yes, she did.

First of all, I don't *fix* my hair. That's what you do when you go to a local beauty shop in the South. You get a new hairdo or get the old one fixed. My hair is groomed, thank you very much. Or styled. Not fixed. It's never been broken, nor does it ever leak. Otherwise, I would summon a plumber or contractor. But Mama qualified my presence with a comment about my hair and my hat. What was next? Public access to my bank account? Honesty.

Southern honesty is charming, refreshing, and comical. You have to laugh at the boldness of these direct remarks, which are not ill-intended but still carry contrary opinion you'd rather not hear, especially when they're made in the presence of an audience. This regional honesty is also endearing because it subtly reflects a nostalgic resistance to change and to newness. The romanticized South is committed to its history and traditions. By nature, its sons and daughters are inclined to suspicion and challenge the concept of change. If you're not convinced, you may recall reading about a domestic dispute commonly referred to as the Civil War.

As affectionately sweet as Southern truths may be, the significant implication is that its native inhabitants are gifted with the ability to regale stories of the past, note observations, and tell tall tales with rich detail and description. This inclination toward such specificity comes from an inherent ability to not only be good observers but to articulate that which they intuit. But the degree to which these kind folks are forthcoming begs for a little less honesty and a lot more embroidery (embellishing for the sake of appearances).

If the Civil War can be remembered as "the time of our most recent unpleasantness," then why can't my hair be similarly described as "the source of *my* most recent unpleasantness?" Will I ever be able to wear pomade without fear of retribution?

Honesty is a good policy. Sometimes, it's just not the best one.

Lost and Found

Whoever coined the phrases, "lost sheep" and "black sheep of the family," wasn't skilled with the ability to use symbolism. To me, the person who stands out in a crowd, marches to the beat of a different drummer, or chooses a lifestyle contrary to the norm is the person I find most interesting. Misunderstood for so many years, two of my uncles, Enoch and Jayroe, were two such mislabeled sheep. Their fleece was anything but black. Their coats were only occasionally tarnished. It comes from weathering life. And neither were they ever lost. My impression is they only strayed from the flock. Enoch and Jayroe deliberately sought pastures they perceived to be greener, but they eventually found their way home.

Enoch Johnson was one of my daddy's older brothers who took great pride in his looks. He kept his hair colored pitch black, used a noticeably greasy tonic to tame it, and listened to country music by artists such as Conway Twitty, Hank Williams, Tammy Wynette, and Donna Fargo. He also liked Pabst Blue Ribbon beer and smoked Pall Mall cigarettes. His personality reflected many things. He was playful and silly. He was a self-professed Casanova. He was also temperamental at times and easily angered if opinion was contrary to his own.

His first marriage ended tragically when his wife, Betty, died of emphysema. She left behind their one and only child—a daughter named Judy. During our younger years, Judy became somewhat of a surrogate sister to my brother and me. We saw her often because she stayed with Grandma Tronie (Daddy's mother) quite frequently. There was a reason she stayed so often. Uncle Enoch had an active social life that was driven by an interest in wine, women, and song. He obviously needed a place for Judy to stay while he was unavailable.

Uncle Enoch and Judy would come down from Wilmington, North Carolina, where they lived, and Judy would be left in Grandma Tronie's care. Our house and Grandma Tronie's house were separated by a tobacco field, and we could easily see who came and went at each other's homes. When I saw Uncle Enoch's green Ford Grand Torino pull up under the pecan trees at Grandma Tronie's, I knew the scenario that would unfold. Uncle Enoch would hand Judy some cash, and off he would go for a weekend of fun and frivolity.

But first, he would take great care in preparing for his weekend of social endeavors. I know this because he groomed himself once at our house, and I watched with great interest. His hair took the most time as he combed, applied tonic, combed some more, and applied more tonic. Once the style was to his liking and he was sufficiently doused in cologne, he yelled to the mirror, "Whooo-weee! Hot damn!" Uncle Enoch was always talking to mirrors. He liked what he saw. Once the reflection approved of the final touches, Uncle Enoch was ready for the weekend. We would see him sometime on Sunday when he would be back to pick up his daughter, and off they would go to their life together.

The relationship between this father and daughter was tumultuous at the very least. Raising a daughter alone while trying to have a grand social life left tons of opportunity for poor parenting. I'm sure his weekly routine reflected a more grownup sense of responsibility because he managed a thriving business. I'm also sure his weekly routine held its share of social carousing that mirrored the weekend sojourns I had chance to witness. He was not in pursuit of any Father of the Year awards. In today's television market, their family dysfunction would have been primo material for debate and discussion on the talk show circuit.

But Uncle Enoch certainly provided for his daughter. He managed a profitable service station and was able to provide Judy with a roof over her head, plenty to eat, and every material thing she could ever want. However, all the material provisions could not compensate for the lack of a solid relationship between the two. For most of their lives, they went back and forth between loving and fighting.

Later in life, Uncle Enoch moved back to South Carolina, managed another gas station in Myrtle Beach, and married a woman less than half his age. His relationship with Judy remained strained, and years would sometimes pass without a word between the two. His second marriage eventually ended in divorce; he retired from the gas station business and he finally settled alone in a quiet, comfortable house near the water. To me, the most interesting thing about this house was when it was built. Uncle Enoch built it rather late in life. His sense of home and security seemed to emerge later rather than sooner.

Ironically enough, just as he was beginning to enjoy a sense of stability and domestic calm, he was diagnosed with cancer and eventually succumbed to the disease. Before he died, I went with Mama and Daddy to visit him. Daddy had fried some fish to take for his dinner. He enjoyed those fried fish, and as he ate, I observed him as carefully as I had that evening many years earlier, when he had meticulously prepared for an evening with the ladies. But on this day, he wasn't preparing for a night of laughs and good times. He was preparing to face his mortality. He seemed at peace. He ate heartily and appreciatively. Though noticeably thinner, his hair was still combed perfectly. He had also reconciled with his daughter to some degree.

The only thing that remained completely unchanged about him was his deformed left hand. It resembled a crab. His thumb and pinky were of normal size. However, the middle three fingers were no longer than a child's toes. When Grandma Tronie was pregnant with Uncle Enoch, she had a dream just days before giving birth to him. She dreamed she was at the beach and casting nets for fish. And in her dream, she was pregnant as well. When the nets were pulled from the ocean, a crab emerged from the net and landed on her protruding stomach. She had no idea what the dream meant. However, days later, Uncle Enoch was born, and his hand bore the reminder of that dream. At the age of sixty-seven, Uncle Enoch died.

◆   ◆   ◆

Jayroe Dawsey, or "Joe," as he was called, was one of Mama's older brothers. He too spent much of his life in pursuit of wine, women, and song. As a member of the U.S. Navy, he served in World War II and was aboard the aircraft carrier, USS Ommaney Bay when it was attacked by the Japanese. The carrier sank, but Uncle Joe survived the attack. He spent the rest of his life trying to survive. At times, "getting by" was all he was able to do, it seemed. He was a gentle soul, but a weak one at times. His vulnerability enabled his wandering lifestyle. His absence of strength seemed to prevent anything of real substance from filling his life.

He fit the stereotype of the quintessential sailor who had disembarked from the ship at a port of call. He held an affinity for a Lucky Stripe cigarette and a stiff drink. He also held an overzealous appreciation for the ladies. Even before his stint in the service, he was rumored to be quite the man about town, as the young girls found his charm intoxicating.

After the war, Uncle Joe came and went in his family's life. He traveled many roads that led to nowhere in particular. As a child, I would see him drift back and forth between nowhere in particular and Grandma Dawsey's house (his mother and my maternal grandmother). One day he would be bunking at Grandma Dawsey's, and the next he would be gone. But wherever he went and whatever he did, we were always grateful he had a bed to come home to at Grandma Dawsey's, if he so desired.

When he wasn't at Grandma Dawsey's house or "nowhere in particular," his primary residence, or "stay place," was in a nearby town with a woman named Cat. I'm sure her name was Catherine, Kathleen, or something similar. But she was always referred to as "Cat." At the time, it seemed appropriate and fitting to refer to her as "Cat," as it implied a less-than-stellar reputation. I don't think I ever saw her in my entire life. She and Uncle Joe were never legally married. Because of the more conservative era in which they cohabitated, she was neither considered a part of the family nor accepted as a legitimate part of Uncle Joe's life. It just didn't seem fittin'. However, she did give him a place to live, and she tolerated the drinking as well as his instability and lack of commitment to anything. And, wherever he went and whatever he did, he similarly had a bed to come home to at Cat's if he so desired. If she got to the point where she had had enough of his ways, out he would go, and to Grandma Dawsey's house he would seek shelter and refuge until it was time to leave again.

Uncle Joe never had a lot of money, as he never held a significant job for any length of time. Once he operated a drive-in that sold the best cheeseburgers I ever tasted. He was actually a great cook, although his penchant for seasoning everything with black pepper was a bit excessive. When I was three years old, I had a case of the chicken pox and was confined to bed. Daddy brought me a cheeseburger from Uncle Joe's drive-in. It was just the right prescription for my ailments. I couldn't believe how good it was. I so hoped his hamburger stand would be open forever, but it wasn't. He was unable to manage it properly, and the business failed—as did many jobs, ventures, and relationships in his life.

Much like Uncle Enoch, Uncle Joe always took great care in grooming his hair. He too was more than generous with the tonic, and he always smelled of Old Spice aftershave. When he was "on the outs" with Cat, the bedroom in which he would sleep at Grandma Dawsey's was affectionately known as the "doll room." I occasionally snuck in there while he was not looking and read through his private collection of books. I learned a great deal about one notorious Madame's promiscuous escapades and trysts throughout Washington, D.C. Uncle Joe was never shy in sharing his own romantic conquests with any of the boy cousins either. We always listened intently while secretly hoping that he would never ask us to elaborate on or compare any of our own personal intimacies.

His relationship with Cat eventually ended. She was finally through with him. By this time, Grandma Dawsey had passed away. Even though her house and the "doll room" were still there for him to use, he only stayed for a brief period and eventually sold the house altogether. I never understood his reason for selling the one place he could always call home. He then spent time on the road while working out-of-town jobs. In between these jobs, he would stay with my Aunt Doe (his sister). As always, he got by and managed to survive.

While staying with Aunt Doe, he met a woman, and they married. He had never been married before, and, to our knowledge, he had no children. He and his new wife settled into a comfortable home located on the Waccamaw River. It was in this new home and during this newfound happiness that he too was diagnosed with cancer.

The salvation in this news was in knowing that he could now fight this new demon with someone by his side and with a place to call home. Uncle Joe did eventually die and was no longer the survivor I had observed through the years. I was in the hospital room when his spirit passed and left the physical earth. The nurse on duty left the room to prepare the paperwork. I was left alone with Uncle Joe. Just him and me. His eyes were still open, and it was the first time I noticed how blue they were. And much like the thirteen-year-old who stood captivated when he spoke of adult subject matter so many years before, I stood in the quiet of that hospital room both afraid and hopeful. Hopeful he might come back to life, and afraid that if he did, he might ask me a question or prompt me to elaborate on some personal intimacy. What a privilege it was to be there as he passed.

There is nothing extraordinary about Enoch Johnson or Jayroe Dawsey. They were two men who struggled with life. Everyone struggles with life. When you consider the tragedies and heartaches other people have endured, Uncle Enoch's and

Uncle Joe's challenges and personal demons paled in comparison. For me, the tragedy was the perception other people may have had regarding these two men. They were probably perceived as men who were morally challenged, men with no regard for discretion, men with no respect for themselves, and men who never mastered the domestic norms set by an era of June and Ward Cleaver vigilantes. During the time they lived, it is likely their lifestyles were perceived as socially unacceptable.

I'm not saying they were traditional role models, but they were memorable to me for many reasons. Because of them, I gained the capacity to understand and accept without judgment—if for no other reason than because they were family. Enoch Johnson and Jayroe Dawsey introduced me to the world of nontraditionalists and nonconformers. I saw them as rebels. They were different.

Sometimes, I feel as if I've been more like each of them more so than anyone else in my family, as I too have chosen a divergent path at times. They both went through a great deal of their lives as single men. They both enjoyed social pursuits. The unknown characterized their lives. And, their hair was always laden with an excess of tonic that I found both stylish and distinctive. I am grateful to them for their adventuresome and nomadic tendencies.

Although I never had a close relationship with either man, my understanding and acceptance of them was both deep and intimate. Regardless of the choices they made, at the end of their respective journeys in life, the only thing mildly different from anyone else was *how* they chose to get there. Their final destinations were and are the same as they are for everyone.

There is someone in practically every family, group, gathering, or community who has been unfortunately misunderstood and similarly mislabeled. As ambassadors of the universally misunderstood and mislabeled, Enoch Johnson and Jayroe Dawsey have enlightened the world with hopeful optimism. These sheep were never really lost. They ventured from the flock, purposefully, and at their own will. And they returned on their own terms, with fleece as white as snow.

Safe Harbors

Daddy used to say that when someone's mind starts to go, it ain't long in this world for that person. It seems as though physical decline becomes more accelerated soon after mental deterioration. He should know. I suppose he saw his share of family members, friends, and neighbors whose old age, sickness, or terminal ailments had induced the loss of full mental functioning and capacity. He would also say, "Once a man, and twice a child." I found it sad and disturbing to see people I knew and loved reverting to either a childlike mentality or living in moments and actions of days past. I felt a loss because I didn't understand the nature of this decline.

However, I've now come to believe this mental regression offers a pathway to safe harbors. It's not a decline, but a step forward in another direction. It is within these states of perceived confusion, disorientation, or childlike tendencies that people actually reclaim the familiar, the comfortable, and the past. It is in these states of mind that they feel safer and find peace.

My daddy's brother, Aubrey Johnson, married Lucille Roberts. She was one of thirty-two children. Her daddy was Mr. Ed Roberts, whom I never knew, but it was my understanding that he fathered all these children by two wives. If you grow up with so many siblings, I'm sure one's personality is influenced by the magnitude of family size. Aunt Lucille certainly had a loving side to her disposition. There wasn't a time when I saw her that she didn't come up to me and want some sugar (i.e., kisses, love, or affection). She was generous with kisses. She would bury her nose just above my ear and inhale deeply. It was as if she was stealing life from me to feed her own soul. She would tell me over and over that I had the sweetest sugar and the sweetest smell. I was more than aware of her capacity to love. Perhaps it was among her enormous family that she inherited this inclination toward affection.

Conversely, when you are one of thirty-two children, the opportunity to lose a sense of one's self must also exist. The instinct to be competitive or protective of limited provisions is understandable. Consequently, there were aspects of Aunt Lucille's behavior that led me to question her degree of happiness and contentment. To use a Southern term, she was "curious acting." Often, I found her to be sullen, jealous, and resentful on occasion. She was always more interested in what someone else had, wanted, or got. For example, if a neighbor got a new car, she would be offended by the extravagance. She would raise an eyebrow to know that someone went out for Sunday dinner rather than staying at home where it was a "whole lot cheaper to eat." The smallest of life's pleasures that other people seemed to enjoy caused her undue concern and worry. I heard people say she got her ways from Mr. Ed, her daddy. Whatever the genetic or environmental source, her behavior led me to believe that happiness was an elusive ideal to her.

She and Uncle Aubrey lived on a farm that sat catty-corner to us and within walking distance, but she came to our house only once in my entire life. It was on the day Neil Armstrong stepped on the moon. It was 1969. She never came again. Uncle

Aubrey would come and visit with us, but not Aunt Lucille. We would see her at church on Sunday. She helped us on our farm a few times during the summer, and we helped her and Uncle Aubrey with their farming at times. Every now and then, we would drive over to their house to visit—even if we just sat on the backdoor steps for a minute. Uncle Aubrey would visit with us and talk. But not Aunt Lucille. She would come out long enough to say "hey," but that was it. I guess she didn't have time to be social. That was another side of her personality: *she was always too busy*.

She was the busiest person I've ever seen: always busy doing something, never a moment's rest. I don't think she ever sat down and thought about life, thought about herself, wondered what was happening in the world, or considered a life other than what she had always known. Did she ever sit down and truly enjoy a meal? Enjoy a song? Enjoy television? Enjoy her family? I don't know. She just seemed too busy to enjoy the fruits of her labor.

There were floors to mop, clothes to wash, animals to feed, yards to clean, meals to cook, and church to attend. She even made her own brooms to sweep the dirt yard behind her house. (A dirt yard is devoid of any grass. It's as hard and smooth as a wood floor and can be swept with the same amount of ease.) She never ran out of something to do. If necessary, she would find something to do, even if it meant picking up an empty bucket sitting on one side of the barn and carrying it to the other side.

And everything she did, she did in haste and with a sense of urgency. Her body language spoke like a soldier at war. She charged. Her shoulders were slightly bent, as if she were sensing danger around the corner. More often than not, if you drove by her house, chances were that you would see her sweeping the dirt yard, walking to the chicken coop to gather eggs, or picking vegetables in the garden during the middle of the hottest day of summer. And she was doing it all with rapid speed. None of this work was imperative. It could have been done in a leisurely manner. Most times, her flurry of activities was not even critical. "Busy doing nothing," as I used to hear Daddy and Uncle Aubrey say. Daddy once said to her, "Lucille, sit down somewhere and get easy 'cause you're always chargin.'" She ignored him and kept going. She never stopped. She was always charging full steam ahead.

Uncle Aubrey died some years ago. With the death of my uncle, the deterioration of Aunt Lucille's own health and mind progressed substantially. She was eventually placed in a nursing care facility. This facility was not an upscale complex with the amenities of a country club. Though pleasant and nice, it was a basic clinical care facility with a dining hall, patient rooms, and recreation area. It reflected the atmosphere of a typical nursing home. When I heard she had been taken to live in this facility, I couldn't imagine how she would be suppressed into living a life of solitude with absolutely nothing to do but stare at the walls, watch television, or commune with other invalids.

For sure, I figured she wouldn't be long for this world. And despite the fact that her mind was no longer what it used to be, I believe that deep down, on some level, she still felt resentment and emptiness—as I perceived she always had. I wondered how she would manage in this transition to a new environment, a new way of living, a new way of coping, and a new way of surviving. Aunt Lucille's mind found an answer. She would keep *busy*. Somewhere, there were chores to be done!

Sometime after Aunt Lucille went to live at the nursing home, Margie Baxley ("Mrs. Margie," as we call her), a long-time friend of our family, was visiting someone at the same nursing care facility. She saw my aunt, and was Lucille Johnson busy! She was cleaning the entire dining hall. She cleared and wiped tables, she swept the floor, she cleaned windows, and she cleaned the seat of every single chair. Mrs. Margie said she had never seen anything like it.

Aunt Lucille was even cleaning the legs of the chairs. During this cleaning chaos, Aunt Lucille happened to see Mrs. Margie and stopped when she recognized a familiar face. Aunt Lucille spoke, "Hey Hattie Mae! How you doin'?" Mrs. Margie replied, "Fine, Lucille. How are you?" Aunt Lucille couldn't tell the difference between Margie Baxley and Hattie Mae Johnson (another of my family's neighbors whom Lucille had also known most of her life). But she knew there was work to be done. She knew to keep busy.

Aunt Lucille's mind had led her to a place of comfort and security. She was busy cleaning. *She was busy doing something.* An escape had been granted. All that she had ever known had somehow resurfaced to grant her the familiarity for which she longed. What her mind had not granted her was complete recollection of those around her. Hattie Mae Johnson was nowhere in the dining hall that day. But a room full of tables and chairs with dusty legs were. Names, faces, family, and friends were no longer critical to surviving this new world in which she lived. Being busy was, and Aunt Lucille found her peace in a cleaning frenzy.

I feel better knowing she discovered her way back to a familiar place—even if it was for just a moment or just an afternoon, however long it lasted. Some people would be convinced that she was truly out of her mind. Crazy, even. She didn't know Margie Baxley from Hattie Mae Johnson, and there she was cleaning the dining hall like a hired janitor. What people might not see or understand is that she found a safe harbor. And in this harbor, the waters were still. There was no storm or chaos. Despite her outward behavior, this vessel was very sound and very capable of navigating.

I am no longer saddened or disturbed by the loss of the spirit I may have once known in others. You see, the spirit isn't lost. It's still there. It docks in safer harbors. And while we may perceive these souls to be adrift at times, their course of direction is familiar, rational, and comfortable—at least to them.

* Lucille Roberts Johnson passed away to even safer harbors on December 14, 2002.

'Cation

It's short for vacation. These days, when I return to visit my family in South Carolina, Daddy always says we're on 'cation, just because I'm home. So, if we go out to have supper at the steak house, or at the local seafood buffet, we're on 'cation. Anything we do, whether it's riding to the Wal-Mart Supercenter Store or sitting and watching television, is considered 'cation time, as long as we're together.

Vacation was something that rarely occurred when I was a child. First of all, Daddy farmed, and the summer was entirely devoted to harvesting tobacco. From the moment school ended in May until the day it started back in late August, there was hardly any opportunity to realistically take time to go somewhere for fun or relaxation. Secondly, it costs money to go on vacation. We weren't poor, but the luxury of a vacation wasn't a priority in our household budget. I can probably count on one hand the number of trips we took that didn't involve visiting a relative. But any trip that included an overnight stay was considered a vacation to me—relatives or no relatives. Regardless of the destination, length of stay, or nature of travel, each little adventure was special and memorable, even though incidence and grandeur were minimal.

The majority of our excursions involved those famous overnight stays at the home of Daddy's one and only sister, Jackie, who lived in Laurens, South Carolina. We would leave early on Saturday morning and return Sunday afternoon. One night was all that Daddy was willing to stay. As he would always say, "I want to be on my own bed tonight. There ain't no bed like my bed." So after the one night's stay, we were off early Sunday morning and back home by early afternoon.

Mama would always fill a Tupperware box full of ham and pimento cheese sandwiches for the trips to Aunt Jackie's house. She would also make sure to have an assortment of salty snacks as side dishes. My favorite was a cracker sandwich where two waffle-style cheese crackers were held together by a ridiculously fattening, processed cheese spread. Daddy would pack a cooler of either "Co-Colas" (that's how we always referred to Coca-Cola) or Pepsi-Colas. We never said "Coke" or "Pepsi." It was either, "Hand me a Co-Cola," or "Hand me a Pepsi-Cola." Diet soft drinks were nonexistent. And, there was always a thermos of coffee reserved for Mama and Daddy. Although neither my brother nor I drank coffee (we were too young), the smell of coffee in a thermos was divine. I couldn't imagine that coffee could possibly taste as good as it smelled.

I couldn't wait to get in the car, regardless of how early in the morning we might be leaving, just to mentally prepare for the presentation of the Tupperware box. And believe me, it was only a matter of minutes before we were asking from the back seat, "Can I have a sandwich?" It's not as if we had never eaten ham or pimento cheese sandwiches before, but the sandwiches made for our little adventure just seemed to smell and taste differently. They were better. We would hardly have driven ten miles before the lid came off that plastic treasure chest, the thermos was opened, and a can of Pepsi-Cola or Co-Cola was passed over the seat. It was official: we were on vacation. Even today, when I eat a ham sandwich, I like to have it with a cup of coffee. It reminds me of those days sitting in the back seat of that Chevrolet Impala, watching Mama pour coffee into a Styrofoam cup and handing it to Daddy along with a ham sandwich.

The overnight stay at my aunt's house was anticlimactic compared to the drive there. For the adults, the visit involved catching up and talking. For me, it was eating. The main event was always suppertime. My aunt was not only a great cook, but she was great with the presentation of the meal. Whether we had a hot dog or barbecue chicken, the table was always set with a tablecloth, silverware, napkins, and placemats. To a little boy who knew nothing about the outside world, the pomp and circumstance of dining at her house was pretty fancy. It rivaled what I had seen on television shows.

The next morning, we were given a big breakfast, the car was packed, and we headed home. We never had a Tupperware full of sandwiches for the return trip. There was no thermos of coffee or cooler of drinks, but it didn't matter. Vacation was over, and it was time for Daddy to get home so he could be on his bed by the end of the night.

Our trips rarely crossed state lines. However, the state of Georgia had occasion to welcome us. We went to Atlanta once to see the Braves play. Aunt Jackie and her family joined us. The game was pretty boring and of little interest to anyone. Because our seats were so high in the stands, Daddy kept saying we could have seen the players better on the television at home. The next day, we drove to the theme park Six Flags Over Georgia, where, for a brief moment, my brother wandered off and got lost in the crowd. The fear of losing a child in a theme park was as scary then as it is now. Fortunately, he was found, and the vacation continued.

The most exciting part of the trip was when we actually stayed in a hotel and not someone's house—something I don't think I had ever done before. It got better. There was a swimming pool. My brother and I got to play in a body of water that wasn't a pond, a river, or the Atlantic Ocean. And we didn't need to wear life jackets (neither of us could swim) because there was a shallow end. I'm sure we had never been in a real pool before—except for the kind you bought at the dime store and filled with water from the backyard garden hose. But there we were, splashing around wearing new swimsuits. We were in a hotel pool. I looked over at Mama who was sitting at a cement patio table. She was watching us play in the water. I encouraged her to come in and join us. I yelled, "Mama, come on in with us!" She continued to sit and responded, "You boys have fun. I'm all right sitting here watching you." That's the way she was, and Daddy, too. Their concern was their children, not themselves.

On our last morning in Atlanta, we stopped at an International House of Pancakes for breakfast. After we had finished and had gotten back on the interstate highway heading for home, Daddy remembered he had left his cap in the restaurant. We had gone too far to turn around and go back for the cap. Leaving the hat behind brought the vacation to a tragic end. To this day, Daddy has no use for IHOP restaurants. If we drive by one, he always says, "I don't care about eating at another one of those damn places again. I left my cap in that one in Atlanta. They'll never get another cap from me!" Of course, he goes on to wonder what happened to that cap and who ended up taking it home to wear. He still thinks that cap is somewhere in Atlanta sitting on somebody else's head or hanging on somebody's hat rack.

Another trip to Georgia to visit Mama's sister in Woodbine (i.e., an overnight's stay) produced yet another interstate highway dilemma. We had stopped at a service station for gas, and Mama proceeded to get locked in the public bathroom. She was locked inside for quite a while. Of course, she would have been freed much sooner had I not been overcome with wonder at the variety of snacks offered in the nearby vending machine. She has never liked public bathrooms for fear of being locked in one, and her worst nightmare came true. I was given clear instructions to wait outside the bathroom until she was finished. Daddy and my brother were across the parking lot fueling the car. I wandered toward the vending machines and became sidetracked. Minutes later, I walked back to the car and got in the front seat. Daddy asked me where Mama was, and I told him I wasn't sure. Maybe the bathroom? We figured it out soon when we noticed a crowd gathering by the restroom area. We also heard quite a noise coming from within the women's bathroom where Mama was—alone.

Between her yelling and banging on the door, a manager was soon summoned, and he was able to finally disassemble the lock. When Mama emerged, she was fit to be tied. She has never been one to use profanity. She even refers to a lady's posterior as her "Alice S. Smith." But without mincing words, she informed the manager that it would serve his best interest to have the *damn* door fixed. She didn't have to say much to me, because I was in tears. I snubbed and sniffled for a few miles once we got back on the highway. Even after we were home and through the years that passed, I stuck close to the bathroom door the few times she had reason to ever frequent public facilities again.

Our little 'cations were nothing grand. We never went anywhere of public acclaim. No national monuments. No historical sites. But they were trips to remember because we were all together. I can't even recall much about some of the places I've been as an adult. I've eaten at much nicer places than the IHOP. I've stayed in luxury hotels. I've traveled in first class. Many of the details regarding these four-star and five-diamond experiences are lost.

My 'cations are far more clear and easy to recall. Because of these 'cations, the taste of ham sandwiches and the smell of coffee in a thermos are not only vivid, but prompt the same level of taste and satisfaction as they did when I was riding in the back seat of our Chevy Impala. My mama still has that Tupperware container in the kitchen drawer, and it is always stocked full with some kind of snack. I continue to think of her every time I stop for gas at freeway service stations. And, I have a fondness for the IHOP restaurant chain, even though Daddy was robbed of his hat.

I'm glad to know that my vacations would appear as nothing out of the ordinary—to most people, that is, except for me. You don't have to travel far for a journey to be worthwhile and full of meaning. If it stays in your heart, the distance traveled is never important. That's how 'cations should be.

Mothers and Nature

A particular television commercial from that turbulent, though sometimes groovy, decade known as the 70s sternly warned the viewing public, "It isn't nice to fool Mother Nature." According to this thirty-second promotional spot, the difference in taste between the new healthier and less cholesterol-laden margarine and that of good old-fashioned, fat-heavy butter was so minimal that even the wisest of souls (i.e., Mother Nature) couldn't tell the two spreads apart. Aside from the margarine-versus-butter taste test, I think television viewers were being gently reminded of a more altruistic message: we should leave Mother Nature alone and, as my mama says, "tend to our own rat killin'." Hmmm...so it seems as though our grand lady of the ecosystem has a way of doing things and taking care of business that is uniquely her own. And while I want to believe that Mother Nature may know how best to care for herself, her home, and her inhabitants, there have certainly been moments and incidents of unexplainable behavior that just don't make sense. To what end could random, irrational behavior render favorable consequences? Is the answer something only a mother would know?

My own mother's history with the forces of nature offers testament of unexplained behavior. It may be helpful to know that Southerners are accustomed to their fair share of natural disasters. Tornadoes and hurricanes tear through the South like Yankee generals on a mission. I can remember suffering through and surviving the winds, lightning, and rain of tornadoes and hurricanes that should have left us homeless and perhaps lifeless. So, in preparation for inclement weather, we took great care to do as the weatherman on Channel 13 in Florence, South Carolina, instructed. We knew to get in a closet doorway, hunker down in the bathtub, or take the appropriate position in the hallway should the wind begin to sound like a locomotive train raring down the tracks. But Mama had her own idea. A very contrary idea. An idea for safety prevention that wasn't remotely rational, logical, and, dare I say, sane?

At the first sound of any wind whipping the pine trees in our backyard or of the house trembling from heavy gusts, she would run to the front door and announce that she was going to run outside and lay down in the frontyard. Daddy would always say, "Are you crazy? What in the hell are people gonna think of you layin' outside on the front grass?" Mama would respond with some random comment of how being outside was safer than being inside, where the ceiling would fall on her. Daddy would then request that she take her rear (that would be her Alice. S. Smith) and get in the hallway with the rest of us. And so, her moment of irrational behavior and careless understanding would pass, and the Johnson's would once again survive a storm sent at Mother Nature's request.

I've often wondered whether Mama's customary threat of running outside and laying in the yard was an unspoken act of defiance that only she could attempt to understand. How could an educated woman, who served for years as a teacher, attempt to explain such incongruent behavior? I won't be too hard on Mama. In her timeline on Earth, she has been a wondrous person. Her occasional misstep in storm preparedness pales in comparison to her otherwise stellar track record.

But what about Mother Nature's occasional missteps? How do you explain earthquakes, fires, flood, and famine? How could such spells of disaster be explained or rationalized? When a tsunami struck the coast of South Asia just one day after Christmas in December 2004, the world practically came to a stop. Under blue skies and without warning, one of Earth's worst natural disasters was set in motion. Ocean waters mysteriously rose and gathered tidal force and speed beyond comprehension. The ripple effect of monstrous waves impacted several countries and millions of lives. *Disastrous* hardly begins to describe the results. Left behind was a state of ruin that exceeded imagination. Human loss abounded. The world was forever changed. What was Mother Nature thinking? I couldn't conceive of any response or reason that would help me understand.

And then, Sybil Gleaton, a friend and a mother herself, offered a rather unexpected insight. I use the word *insight*, because she was adamant that it was not her intention to offer an answer. A Christian, whose faith in God is both steadfast and refreshingly progressive, Sybil reminded me that the Earth takes care of itself in ways that we couldn't possibly understand or justify. Mother Nature, though brutal and harsh at times, must purge and cleanse so that balance is maintained or restored. Sybil continued by saying that during Mother Nature's timeline of evolvement and progression, a course of development has been followed that appears rational and sound if you look at the "big picture." Behavior that defies convention, challenges our faith, and begs our understanding is more uncommon than common. Sybil concluded by encouraging me to consider Mother Nature's since-the-beginning-of-time track record—a remarkable track record despite an occasional lapse in judgment.

I'm not sure that I was completely satisfied with the insight she offered, but I found some sense of comparative resolution within her words. Mothers and Mother Nature have their particular ways of caring for those and that which are their own. Neither their tenure nor their track record should be judged by a single, occasional lapse in judgment. Consequently, I no longer wonder why Mama had the need to run outside during a storm. And now, I am less prone to question that which Mother Nature may impose upon us. And if I still need to question *Why,* I resolve to believe that the answer is something only mothers would know.

More, Most, and the Mostest

No one needs to explain to me the grammatical rules governing the use of the comparative *more* and the superlative *most*. I understand the context in which each word should be technically applied. It's really simple. One is a relevant degree of the other. I just don't understand why they are used sometimes. Especially when the opposing descriptives, *less* and *least*, are more apropos. English books seem to ignore this unintended irony. In other words, whether the statement is accurate or true is irrelevant as long as grammatical rules are clearly followed. My daddy wouldn't receive passing marks on his word choice, but he excelled in interpretation. He once said, "Some people have done the damned near *leastest* to appear to have done the *mostest*." Accurate terms, incorrect usage.

Many, many years ago, I was sitting in the fellowship hall of the church I attended one hot, humid Sunday afternoon. A potluck supper was being held for some reason, and each family attending was responsible for bringing a fully cooked meal in order to make sure there was enough food available for their respective family as well as any visitors or guests in attendance. As each family came into the fellowship hall, the mothers and wives led each family's procession with the main courses, as children, fathers, and husbands followed with outstretched arms of homemade fixins'. The tables were full of all the good things that create the stereotypical Southern feast. And on the counter by the kitchen sink, row upon row of Styrofoam cups were waiting to be filled with sweetened tea. And when the tea is poured, at least in the South, it's time for the blessin' (prayer) and then the meal.

It was during the final words of "It's time to fix ya' plates and eat" that a last-minute guest arrived: a Jell-O mold. I could not believe what I saw. An upstanding member of the church came hurriedly through the doors carrying a single Jell-O mold. That's all. Not an apple pie. Not a chicken potpie. Not a pot of chicken and rice. Not even rice pudding. This was a Jell-O mold that I swear to this day was purchased at the Piggly Wiggly.

When that Jell-O mold came walking in the fellowship hall, you would have thought the second coming of Christ was taking place. Moses did less when he parted the Red Sea. Everyone made such a fuss over the grandeur of this Jell-O mold. It wasn't as if any amount of time had really been put into making it, preparing it, or even buying it from the Piggly Wiggly. And more than anything else, it was Jell-O, an insult to the Southern palette. But everyone in the church fellowship hall practically came to a halt in honor of the contribution this one lady made with a Jell-O mold. Because she was a fine, upstanding, and popular member of the congregation, I suppose anything she did was viewed with reverence. However, if that Jell-O mold had arrived in the company of anyone else, a public lynching would have been held. At the very least, repentance before God would have been needed. It wouldn't be the last time I would have occasion to witness or experience such a degree of inconsistency between perception and reality.

My first job upon completing graduate school allowed me the opportunity to learn even more about Jell-O molds. After a number of years with this company, I was placed under the supervision of an employee who was newly hired. It took very little time for my intuition to be confirmed. I believed a Jell-O mold was among us. The time spent working with this associate eventually created many tense, stressful, and uninspiring moments for me.

For months, I was amazed how little work this person did compared to the high level of praise received. On paper, the accolades were astonishing. Revenues increased. The client base began to grow. The portfolio of products and services offered were enhanced. Of course, very little of the success had anything to do with this supervisor. Some of it was luck. Some of it was simply timing. The façade created a picture of behind-closed-doors meetings, lots of phone calls, stacks and stacks of papers sitting on the desk, executive luncheons, and hurried mannerisms. It all looked very busy. There was no substance to any of it. But you can believe this person was more than compensated and recognized for the successes within the department.

As time passed, I was eventually placed under the direct supervision of another company officer, and I was no longer accountable to someone who I perceived as having no concept of accountability. The new situation didn't offer any real benefit other than that it allowed me to view the Jell-O mold from a new perspective and a new angle. Unsurprisingly, the mold continued to hold perfect shape and form. That's how Jell-O molds are if they're well protected, kept from direct heat, and are allowed to sit without being disturbed. They can actually last a very long time.

The particular employee I reference continued working at the company for some time after I left my position. But, this person also eventually resigned and accepted another more lucrative position with an even more prestigious organization. I can only assume the more attractive offer was based on a perceived track record of accomplishment and success. In reality, to have seemingly done so much, this person had done very little.

It happens all over the world. Everyday. To VIPs. To everyday people. Across every profession. Having worked in the entertainment field, I've known actors who never work, yet their talent is incredible. Unfortunately, the closest they will ever come to success or stardom is in front of their televisions, where less-talented performers—accepting awards, receiving acclaim, and walking red carpets, no less—are featured. There are office workers in administrative and management positions that will experience the incompetence of peers and supervisors, just as I did. Revenues will increase, bottom-line profits will soar, and financial history will be made as the least-deserving worker receives the undeserved credit.

And finally, consider the Jell-O mold-turned-skydiver who jumps from a plane; a parachute emerges and a safe, uneventful landing occurs. Then consider the skydiver whose parachute fails after jumping from a plane and the skydiver is forced to sew a makeshift parachute while landing in burning fires over enemy territory. Want to take a guess at who might be recognized for heroic acts of courage and who might not?

Injustice is just nonsense. I'm sorry. It ain't right. Because I fall under the astrological sign of Libra, it's my nature to find balance, justice, cause and effect, and a favorable fairness ratio in every situation. The worst part is that injustice ain't goin' away. But there is some good news. Most of these overestimated wonders of the world represent the minority. The majority includes those of us who work, toil, contribute, and give with a strong belief that our blessings, treasures, and rewards are forthcoming. And should these compensations fall short or fail to present, we still continue to work, toil, contribute, and give.

Being in the majority means we're not alone. So, there's comfort in numbers. We all experience these frustrating situations. And no matter how unbelievable the circumstances may seem, someone else in the office down the hall or in the office building next door is similarly enduring and tolerating.

I have no doubt there are a few more Jell-O molds in my future. There will be someone who "has done the damned near *leastest* to appear to have done the *mostest*." Nothing should surprise me at this point. Daddy warned me a long time ago. He was accurate if nothing else.

A Table Full

I can proudly say I have never been hungry—for anything. In addition to good groceries, the provisions of attention, love, and affection were all equally abundant in my childhood. If a kitchen, in any way, reflects the bounty in one's life, my family was richly blessed with almost embarrassing wealth. And I'm not talking about fancy cars, swimming pools, designer clothes, or extravagant vacations. I mean to say the kitchen cabinets were stocked full of snacks, goodies, and fillers of almost every kind. There were leftovers of some sort usually sitting out on the counter from the previous meal. The deep freezer was packed with meats and vegetables raised and grown on our farm. And come mealtime, there was always plenty on the table when we sat down to eat. Plenty to feed our stomachs. Plenty to feed our hearts and souls. There was always a table full of nourishment.

My mama has always been a great cook. She knows how to put on a spread. I followed her enough times up and down every aisle at the Piggly Wiggly grocery store to know she had a handle on what she was doing. And then I watched her wrangle the pots and pans with such aplomb that anything short of delicious was not possible. She has cooked under pressure. She has cooked with short notice. She has cooked for the masses. She has cooked for the preacher.

Daddy has his own way of filling the table. I've watched him kill hogs, hang them over large steaming wash pots or iron kettles, and procure the most enjoyable pork meat I've ever tasted. I've seen him prepare salt-cured hams in the smokehouse. He's raised cattle for food, and he's fished for food. He's planted the most beautiful gardens, which flourished with every imaginable vegetable that would dare grace a suppertime table.

Together, he and Mama have always provided generously. But as a child, it was more than food that garnished our kitchen table. When we sat down to eat, we were together. And without knowing it then, we were being filled with a sense of family and belonging. Everyone knew what the other had done that day. Everyone knew what was happening tomorrow. My brother and I were never begged or ordered to come and eat. We were glad to be there. Neither debate nor compromise was necessary to guarantee our presence at the table. We were there. And our parents were there with us and for us.

However, there is a slight disadvantage to such fond recollections. The tendency for anyone to compare a wonderful childhood memory of what they cherish to anything else is sometimes like comparing apples to oranges, or apples to less-ripe apples. When I was once invited to join a couple at their home for dinner, I looked forward to seeing their home, meeting their children, and being a part of their family's evening meal. The first thing I noticed was the pantry in disarray. Bags of potato chips and pretzels had been left open with their contents littered on the floor. Two loaves of bread had both been eaten from and left unsecured. Candy bars, half-eaten and still in the wrappers, lined the shelves. Duplicate containers of all kinds of cooking supplies (oil, sugar, seasonings, etc.) sat randomly about the shelves without any organization. I counted at least four cans of PAM nonstick cooking spray at four different locations in the pantry. Nothing substantial could have been obtained from all that was seemingly available. It may as well have been empty.

The meal seemed to mirror the pantry's belongings. The table was a mishmash of several different kinds of foods, including Chinese food, Lucky Charms cereal, pizza, and Pop-Tarts. The selection of various cuisines was necessary because each child liked and disliked certain foods. And even with the tailor-made menus, the children were threatened and coerced in an effort to have them sit and eat. When that didn't work, they were promised toys, trips, and video games. Debate, compromise and resolution worthy of the United Nations dominated the chaotic beginnings. But once everyone was seated, the meal finally commenced.

You could have heard a pin drop. Not a person spoke. I observed the dynamics carefully as each person dropped his or her head and ate in silence. No one had any idea what the point of being together meant. The concept of talking was not entertained. They didn't know how to behave around each other in this intimate situation. The children were not even accustomed to sitting and conversing during the meal. The silence was disturbing, but thankfully short-lived. The meal was over in less than fifteen minutes. We were finished. Place settings had been beautifully arranged at the table. A more-than-adequate amount of food, representing several different tastes, had been prepared and was available. Six people sat around the table together, yet the table was empty.

In 1950, my mother was a freshman at Lander College, a then small, private institution in upstate South Carolina. She was fortunate enough to have an academic scholarship, because she didn't come from a wealthy family. She would be the first to say her family was poor. Everybody in those days was poor, but her family always had plenty to eat, clothes to wear, and a clean home. They also knew what it meant to sit down together over a meal and share as a family. It was during Mama's freshmen year at Lander that she was invited to spend a holiday weekend at the home of a young woman who had become her friend. Mama was glad to have somewhere to go rather than spend a long weekend alone in the dormitory. They took a bus to the girl's hometown, where her father met them.

They rode in an old truck to her friend's house. Mama recalls the house being very rundown and weathered. They walked into the kitchen where Mama found very sparse furnishings. A long wooden table with wooden benches on each side filled the center of the room. An old wood stove, which sat in the corner, and a single cabinet nailed to the wall, completed the remaining décor. On the stove was a pot of lima beans that had been cooking. On the table were a pan of cornbread and a bottle of ketchup. No one spoke. They simply sat down and ate.

The minimal provisions and stark surroundings were interrupted briefly when a young girl, deformed and retarded, appeared out of nowhere. Mama's friend jumped from the table and ushered the girl away. The moment was awkward as was the mood in the home. Nothing was ever said about this girl, the meager offerings, or the weekend spent together. Mama was embarrassed for her friend. The physical environment of the kitchen in which she ate offered a glimpse into the life of this family, and it had nothing to do with the lack of furnishings or the minimal food provisions. The room reflected a certain loneliness. The long wooden table was designed to accommodate more than this family could offer. Something was missing. The table was empty.

Kitchens, pantries, and dinner tables come in all shapes, sizes, and designs. These structural resources are engineered to support food preparation and consumption. People rely on these domestic components to eat and survive. But most importantly, these items help make a house a home. In more ways than we know, they feed those who dwell within. The dynamics of a family can be found in its kitchen. Take a look in the cupboard, the cabinets, or the refrigerator. See what kind, if any, of paper lines the shelves. Is the kitchen table used for storage or fellowship? Is mealtime reconciling or divisive? Is the table prepared so that the family is nourished?

Being undernourished, either physically or emotionally, has never been a concern to me. I have lived a very fortunate and privileged life in that regard. Ironically, in a world where people still die from starvation, my concern has always been whether I've eaten too much. And I have. But if you had sat at Mama and Daddy's table when it came time to eat, you'd be full too. There was plenty of *everything* to go around, and we all had second helpings most times.

To Cull, or Not to Cull

Daddy, my brother, and I were sitting at a diner in Lake City, South Carolina, one summer day. We had just come from delivering a load of tobacco at the warehouse and had stopped to get supper. As the waitress was setting the plate in front of Daddy, she realized that something about his food wasn't prepared as it had been ordered. Before she could apologize and attempt to right the wrong, he stopped her and said, "Don't you worry, honey. Set it right here. I don't *cull* it." In other words, he ain't particular when it comes to food. He added, "I'm just glad to get it." The disposition of *need* versus *want* has been clear in my mind ever since.

We've seen the news reports. We've read the articles. We've been solicited by the charitable organizations. Each medium desperately pleads for increased awareness and support for world hunger, for financial and humane assistance to those who are perishing. The visual of Third World citizens standing in line for a ration of porridge or rice came humbly to my mind as I waited for coffee one day. I too was standing in a long line—at Starbucks. A line for decaf mochas, soy lattes, Frappucinos, and the privilege of preference and abundance. Time zones and cultures away, another kind of line in another kind of country was driven that same day by survival and desperation. For me, the primal difference between the two lines of people and two worlds of culture boiled down to the mentality that separates the "haves" from the "have-nots." One is prone to culling. The other has no idea what *culling* means.

For the record, if you cull it, it means you're picky or selective—and not necessarily in a good way. You hem and haw over what's given to you, and you turn your nose up. The reasons for people being picky are as legitimate as the reasons other people aren't. But in the end, you either cull it, or you don't. I once refused to drink from a Co-Cola bottle that someone else in my family had opened. Daddy scolded me and said to stop being Mr. Nice Nasty. His comment somehow referenced my hesitancy to drink from the same bottle for fear of germs. Obviously, I wasn't very thirsty, otherwise I would have taken a drink from the bottle. But I had culled it. Anytime he sees somebody "turn up their nose" at the food that's cooked and put in front of them, he says, "You ain't been hungry yet." He's right. People who must stand in line for rations know what it feels like to be hungry. They will never "turn up their nose" at the chance to eat. They will never be in a position to decline or pass on the offerings. They will never cull it.

Except for the time I behaved like Mr. Nice Nasty, I consider myself to be one who isn't picky. I'm among the "haves" insomuch as I've never been without food. But even with all that I've had, I still ascribe to my daddy's less-demanding parameters when it comes to selection and preference. If it's cooked, I'll pretty much eat it. High levels of culinary skill and gourmet tendencies are delightful but not required. As a rule of thumb, I would prefer a more healthful menu; however, if somebody goes to the trouble of cooking and preparing a meal for me, I won't cull it. It doesn't matter if it's fried, steamed, broiled, boiled, or burned. I'm gonna fall in on it.

The same goes for Daddy. He's always been among the "haves" when it comes to plenty of food. He wasn't raised in a life of luxury. His family, which included seven boys and a girl, lived on a farm and led a less-than-easy lifestyle. They bordered on poverty, much like most families in the era of the Depression. He grew up with outdoor plumbing; his mama cooked on a woodstove; and they didn't have electricity until he was almost eighteen years old. His family's home burned down when he was eleven years old, and they lost everything they had. Adversity was not unfamiliar to them or many of the families during that time and age.

As a young boy on a big farm, he plowed a lot of fields with a mule and harness. There were no tractors. No heavy-duty farm machinery. Nothing but a lot of work. And when suppertime rolled around, he was ready for it. In describing his childhood, he was always thankful: "We had plenty to eat, and we were glad to get it."

While in college, I worked a summer job as manager of a waterslide in Myrtle Beach, South Carolina. Each day, two little girls, who lived very near the water park, arrived with their towels and sunscreen. Their mother dropped them off in the morning and picked them up in the afternoon. What I began to notice very soon was that they rarely ate. I also noticed they wore the same swimsuits every day—swimsuits that were tattered and worn.

One day, I noticed them sitting at a picnic table near the snack bar. They watched other children and families come and go with hot dogs, ice cream, potato chips, and sodas. To their surprise, I appeared out of nowhere with two ice cream cones. I sat down and talked with them. They lived alone with their mama, who worked two jobs. There was little money in the household. By leaving the girls at the waterslide each day, the mother was able to avoid excessive childcare expenses. They rarely saw their daddy and didn't know where he lived.

On a typical day, their mama gave them cereal for breakfast, and they usually didn't eat again until supper that night. Occasionally, I would see them eating a piece of fruit, but most times they sat and watched other people eat. But from the day I talked with them until my last day at work, they did eat between breakfast and supper. I saw to it. The first time I bought them lunch, they had no idea what to make of the food. I had purchased hamburgers and French fries from a restaurant nearby. The youngest girl actually became sick with an upset stomach. I figured she wasn't used to rich, heavy meals. But she got used to it. I was determined to make sure they wouldn't be hungry. And like Mama or Daddy had told me all my life, "If I eat, you eat." Whatever I fed those two little girls that summer, they didn't cull it. They were glad to get it.

My brother, Eric, once taught school and coached athletics in a town where the socioeconomic status was skewed toward lower-income levels and a large ethnic population. As both a teacher and coach, he was as giving and caring to his students and teams as I was to those two little girls in Myrtle Beach. On most occasions, his compassion was generously lavished on children whose home life was impoverished and who survived on minimal provisions. He went above and beyond the duties outlined in his job description.

My parents also joined him in his efforts to help provide some relief and momentary joy to these kids. Mama and Daddy went to almost every game my brother coached and supported his players as if they were their own children. Most of these kids were poor. The idea of going to McDonald's after a game to get something to eat was not taken for granted. To have a couple of dollars to buy a hamburger was a rarity. Consequently, my parents would sometimes give the players money so they could stop and eat. Other times, Mama would have snacks and sandwiches for the players once the game was over.

On one particular occasion, Mama made peanut butter and jelly sandwiches. When the game was finished and the players were preparing to go home, she handed them all a sandwich. She noticed one particular young man who stuck the sandwich in his pocket. She was afraid he didn't like peanut butter and jelly and asked him whether he would have preferred something else. He told her he was saving the sandwich for the next morning. By saving it, his little brothers would have something to eat for breakfast. They would be glad to get it. And I can bet you they didn't cull it.

I have an ongoing joke with my sister-in-law, Jena. She once attempted to tell me what kind of bacon she liked best. I stopped her before she even got detailed with her preferences of crispness and leanness. I interjected, "The kind that's cooked and put in front of you." She laughed, while immediately realizing she had set herself up for a punchline. Everyone knows that the best tasting food is the kind you don't have to cook yourself! Always the good sport, she is quick to note the underlying message behind my comment that day. I appreciated her sense of humor, and I hope she appreciated my not-so-subtle yet humble reminder of what our most basic needs are.

I find humility in hunger. To know that people in our country and in the world are without reminds me of how insignificant I am. Self-regard that is anything but modest would be offensive. Especially when those who are at the mercy of others feel insignificant themselves. It is the "have-nots" who should be held in high regard. The nobility of withstanding deprivation is heroic. I can't empathize with the less fortunate, as I have no idea what it is to be hungry. But, I can appreciate and be grateful for what's cooked and put in front of me—not because I know what it's like to have been without, but, ironically, because I know the privilege of choice, preference, and abundance.

So when it was my time to order at Starbucks, I simply asked for a cup of black coffee. No half-decaf/half-regular, no two-percent milk vs. whole milk, no one pack of Sweet'N Low whipped, not stirred. Just black coffee. And if for some reason I would have gotten anything other than what I ordered, I would have kept on going, because I don't cull it.

Dear Santa

December 24, 2002

Christmas wish lists and the people who write them are a lot alike. Over the course of time, they both change: from bicycles to blenders, from blenders to memories of Christmas past, from childhood to parenthood, and from parenthood to memories of Christmas past.

Tonight is Christmas Eve, and I am with Mama and Daddy. I am always home for Christmas. In my entire life, I have neither been with anyone else nor been anywhere else this time of year. I'm always at home with them. My brother is with his wife and children. They'll come to Mama and Daddy's tomorrow, and we'll celebrate together. But tonight, it's just the three of us.

I'm the last to go to bed. The folks have been asleep for some time. One of them is snoring. I peak in their room, and all I see are two motionless mounds of bedding and linen. Neither of them stirs. I can safely bet there will be no clandestine activity during the middle of the night in order to offer proof that Santa Claus was here. It's almost the New Year, 2003. Not, 1973. Hence, no toys will be left by the Christmas tree for surprised eyes to see. No snacks have been left on the kitchen table for an after-hours "do-gooder" who ventures inside the house with a sack full of toys. No Christmas morning debris, including an empty Co-Cola bottle and paper plate, will be strategically scattered in the driveway to demonstrate Santa's carelessness in dashing away.

Times have changed. So while Mama and Daddy sleep soundly, it's just *The Weather Channel* and me. Me and a passing low-pressure system that has produced partly cloudy skies, mild temperatures and slight precipitation. The yuletide routine isn't the same as it was thirty years ago. I'm not the same as I was thirty years ago. And, my wish list is much different than it was thirty years ago.

My letter to Santa Claus doesn't ask for a new basketball. No sense in getting a portable phonograph. No interest in a cell phone or laptop computer. My wish to Santa Claus is to just be home for Christmas next year with my family. And the year after. And the year after. I'm not sure I would ever be satisfied being here at Mama and Daddy's house without them. The inviting sense of home would be missing. Food wouldn't taste the same. The house wouldn't smell the same. The same brown paneling, the same pictures, the same recliners, and the same floral arrangements, which have shared residence all these years, just wouldn't be the *same*. The worst part about being home at Christmas without my parents? If it's just *The Weather Channel* and me, it means I'm alone. And if I'm alone, it means I'm no longer someone's child. I'm no one's son anymore. I no longer belong to anyone.

During the course of our lives, we assume many roles that seemingly define who we are. Job titles, social positions, and romantic relationships consume our time and require commitment. These roles detail and outline both responsibilities and entitlements. And regardless of the role, each necessitates a status level or label. But, it is the status as *child* that implies an inherent claim to belonging. Sons and daughters belong to mothers and fathers: all over the world, in times past, and in times to come.

In a world rife with conflict, despair, turmoil, and fear, one of the greatest sources of strength is a sense of belonging. In a world equally filled with miracles, magic, and wonder, one of the greatest joys is the ability to celebrate with those who share our lives. To celebrate with those to whom we belong.

For when we belong, we have access to guardianship and safekeeping. As long as we remain someone's child, we live in the safe shadows of those who accept our shortcomings, imperfections, disappointments, joys, successes, and triumphs as their own. As children, life's journey is less the challenge because parents provide the ease and comfort of transition and progress. As long as we remain someone's child, we belong and we are never alone.

Though complicated, my wish list is short. Surely, St. Nick can figure out the logistics of filling my stocking with an eternal wish: *to remain my parents' son and to always belong.* Delivery of this special wish shouldn't be a problem for Santa and his reindeer this night. According to *The Weather Channel,* a high-pressure system is moving into the area later in the evening. Clear skies are forecast.

And You Are?

"Tell me about yourself." I might as well be asked, "What is the meaning of life?" I've never had an insightful, provocative response for the first directive. And regarding the question that follows, all I have to say is this: if *Webster's Dictionary* hasn't elaborated any more than what it says on page 827 of Mama and Daddy's new revised edition, then you're asking the wrong feller, 'cause I don't know what life means. But, I did hear a couple of insightful comments that may resolve both of these inquiring generalizations—at least for me.

I'm not sure whether Mama was offended or afraid, or whether she thought I had completely lost my mind. I called to check in on her and Daddy one afternoon, and I happened to be in one of those freewheeling moods. After all the pleasantries were swapped, after I had been updated on who had died recently, and after I had been advised of the latest weather conditions, I decided to pose a personal query to Mrs. Johnson (Mama).

I didn't think I was completely in left field. Mama is very educated. She was the valedictorian of Aynor High School's class of 1950. She graduated from college in less than four years with high grades and proceeded to teach school for almost forty years. And if that's not enough, she watches *Oprah* and *The View*. So I propositioned her, "Tell me who you are, Shirley

Johnson. What are your hopes and dreams?" I wasn't trying to quiz her in case she somehow made it to the finals of a beauty pageant, was asked to wait fretfully in the isolation booth, and then answer a judge's final question. I thought my question was harmless enough. I thought she would at least have some type of answer. I thought wrong.

I might as well have asked her to pull her pants down. She laughed nervously and wanted to know what was wrong with me. I persisted. "Who are you, really?" She replied with another frightened giggle of apprehension before asking me again what in the world was wrong with me. Before I knew it, she had handed the phone over to Daddy without even notifying me that our conversation was over.

So Daddy takes the phone and asks me what I want to know. I explain to him that I simply asked Mama who she was, what her dreams are, and so on. Silence ensued. I asked him to tell me who he is. His response was quick, confident, and unesoteric: "I reckon I'm the same damn person I've been for seventy-two years." Well, whip out the smellin' salts. You could have knocked me over with a feather. He answered me. And he answered me truthfully and profoundly. There was nothing about his answer that needed explanation. Whoever he is, he's the same. He defined himself as consistent. What more could you want?

To him, there was no difference between who he used to be and who he is. There was only a passage of time. Although Daddy may have you think he's a seventy-two-year-old soul, everyone goes through transitions and metamorphoses. They change. They evolve. We all have to, because life invites, challenges, and often demands that of us. We may feel as though we're the same person we once were, but seldom is that the case. However, at the core of our souls is a genetic strain that continues, unaltered, through each stage of our development. This strain carries the true essence—character, if you will—of who we are. And as we each begin our respective journeys in life, this core nucleus of properties goes with us.

Yes, there have been changes in Daddy. Changes that he may not see or realize, but changes nonetheless. However, at the center of who and what he is, the nucleus has remained untouched. Robert B. Johnson is still Robert B. Johnson. Seventy-two years ago. Last year. Yesterday. Today. Tomorrow. And next year.

And what about the meaning of life? I wish I could say one of my parents takes the credit for providing my favorite response to this age-old question. But, alas, it was a woman named Rose, who has always had a quick wit and ability to tell it like it "*tiz*." I had joined Rose, along with a few other friends, at a local country bar where the discussion paralleled much of the lyrics we were hearing in the songs being played: heartache, heartbreak, cheatin', lovin', fightin', and more heartache. What better place to discuss such painful woes? After all, country music solves most of life's problems. And so, I asked, "What is the meaning of life?" Although it was rhetorical, I figured if anyone would have an answer to this question, Rose would. And if she didn't, she'd know somebody who did. She had an answer. And I got told. I got told good.

Unlike many Southerners, Rose has the unique ability to be concise when making a remark or telling a story. Her monologues are not long-winded or exhausting. She has no need to preface a conversation with the family lineage of the person in question, when she last saw the person at Wal-Mart, and whose new Buick has been sitting in this person's front yard for over a week.

On the evening I spent with Rose and some other friends, her knack for brevity was still fully intact. And perhaps because of an overindulgence in her favorite libation, she was forthcoming with several kernels of wisdom across a diverse range of subjects. But when challenged to define the meaning of life, everything else she had said all evening paled in comparison.

When Rose heard the question asked, she retaliated with an initial response of impatience and finished with a statement of confident brilliance: "What does it matter what life means? You just get through it the best damn way you can." The remark was sobering. I agreed. Does life have to imply anything? Does it have to offer a universal standard of rhyme or reason? Does it have to be specific? Definitive? Relative? Comparable? Not according to Rose. You're given life—now live it, no questions asked. Go about the business of each day, each month, and each year with whatever purposeful intent you feel is necessary or needed for your own situation. For your own set of circumstances. For your own life.

At the time I write this book, let me say, *"I reckon I'm the same damn person I've been for forty years, and I get through life the best damn way I can."* And you are?

Life. Be There at Ten 'Til.

Reader's Guide

Life. Be There at Ten 'Til.

A town clock becomes less an instrument of time and more a reflection of one's character. A lazy farm dog finds his way home and reminds us that there is something to learn in the routine and minutia of everyday life. Two birthday parties, two birthday girls, and one insightful journey from the East Coast to the West collectively fashion and tailor the circle of life's tapestry. In the early hours of a summer morning, stars and eggs become faithful reminders of comfort and safety. A cedar chest and a cubbyhole champion simplicity, the less-is-more approach to achieving life's happiness. And this is just the beginning.

Such are the images, visuals, and real-life, honest-to-goodness situations that navigate one young man's journey from childhood to the present. And from these unassuming and ordinary inspirations come a bounty of wisdom and learning as this Southern native who now lives in Hollywood ventures through time in recounting poignant vignettes and stories with powerful, life-affirming payoffs. Although the South figures prominently in this unique and inspirational soul-searching expedition, the boundaries of geography give way to universal insight, understanding, and appeal.

- **Life. Be There.**—Don't just show up for life; get there early. You'll be all the wiser.

- **Creatures of Habit**—A family pet returns to the fold and reminds us that ironically enough, inspiration can be found within the mundane, predictable, and uninspiring patterns of life.

- **Birthday Girls**—Two very different birthday parties remind us of both the celebration and passing of life.

- **A Cedar Chest and a Cubbyhole**—Defining and valuing wealth becomes as simple as remembering childhood possessions.

- **Stars and Eggs**—The gifts of care and comfort are realized in the dark of an early summer morning.

- **Growing Up in Payless**—Defining moments can happen anywhere—even in a shoe store.

- **Can You Dig It?**—Years after retiring from a stellar teaching career, a mother is finally acknowledged for her contribution And is formally bestowed life's most noble virtue.

- **Twinkle, Twinkle, Little Star**—From stars in the sky to stars in Hollywood, sometimes it's best to just admire stellar things from afar.

- **Greater Than, Less Than**—A second grade teacher's arithmetic lesson offers humanity the hope for equality.

- **Toughskins**—A clothing label offers hope and understanding as its brand name becomes applicable to the person and not the garment.

- **The Need to Know**—Being curious ain't just Southern, it's inherited. It's in the DNA.

- **World's Finest**—A popular candy bar prompts reflection on the worldwide human condition.

- **Easy as Pie (and Ham)**—Balance may be found in a dessert ritual.

- **Fear Not. God Is Great; God Is Good.**—Embracing God or any type of spirituality should be liberating and free— and more than anything, free from fear.

- **Southern Comfort**—Southern food truly is not only the way to one's heart but to one's sense of humility.

- **The Better Policy**—A favorite aunt offers surprising proof that honesty may not be the best policy.

- **Lost and Found**—Two "black sheep" uncles return to the fold to offer powerful perspective.

- **Safe Harbors**—An aunt begins to regress mentally but offers solace in facing decline and mortality.

- **'Cation**—You don't have to travel far for vacations to be memorable. If they stay in your heart, the distance travelled is never important.

- **Mothers and Nature**—For the occasional misstep by Mother Nature and mothers alike, there just may be a method to the momentary madness.

- **More, Most, and the Mostest**—The mystery of undeserving praise is resolved through coworkers, churchgoers, and parachuters alike.

- **A Table Full**—A suppertime table is filled with nourishment as plenty of food and plenty of love guarantee second helpings.

- **To Cull or Not to Cull**—The humility of hunger is found in the art of "culling."

- **Dear Santa**—A grown-up wish list for Santa includes just one seemingly small yet infinite plea.

- **And You Are?**—Defining one's self and one's life may be easier than you think.

From the tobacco fields in South Carolina to red carpet premieres in Hollywood, the memories recounted are steeped in rich storytelling tradition with real family members and friends full of charm, personality, and lessons to share. The stories make readers intimately familiar with the characters. From Mama and Daddy and an only brother to an extended family of grandparents, aunts, uncles, cousins, and friends galore, R. Dean Johnson's retrospective guide to enlightenment boasts a cast of people that are so universally familiar that you'll begin your own journey of soul searching. Each of these wonderful real-life personalities has a counterpart in people we all know somewhere in the world. And from them we continue to learn, gain wisdom, and grow.

Twenty-five chapters. Twenty-five refreshing commentaries on life. And in between are back roads, interstate highways, side trips down memory lane, and all the expected thrills, joys, disappointments, and possible sorrows that a typical family vacation (or *'cation* as revealed in one chapter) may entail. Of course, the saddest part of any adventure is when the end is near and the final destination is in sight. Yet the final chapter offers hope that the journey isn't ending at all. It may just keep going—only in another direction.

An Interview with R. Dean Johnson

1) How does the element of time figure into the title of your book and to the overall message your book imparts?

I wasn't sure exactly how I would take twenty-five chapters and decide upon one global title that captured the essence of the book. Each chapter imparts a unique wisdom, a new understanding, or a fresh way of looking at life's most basic lessons; so I simply decided to pick one chapter title to represent the whole book. "Life. Be There." became the flagship message, and hence the title was assigned to the book as well as the first chapter. However, the title still needed flavor and substance, so I went within the chapter itself and extracted the icing on the cake.

Let me explain. Located about fifteen miles from the farm where I grew up is the town of Conway, South Carolina. In front of the local police department stands the town's beautiful and historical clock. My daddy always loved that clock and used it in his parental instruction when reminding my brother and me of the virtues of being on time. He used to say, "If I tell a man I'm gonna meet him at the town clock at 1 PM, I'm gonna get there at ten 'til." In other words, show up, be on time, and be accountable. The words speak volumes on so many levels. Show up for life. Show up for relationships. Show up for your career. Be there, and be in "it" all for the long haul, and let your character speak of accountability and responsibility to yourself, to others, and to the world around you.

2) You mention in your book that you have a brother. Does he recall these memories from your childhood as you do? If so, is his recollection the same or different and why?

My brother, Eric, wrote me a letter after he read the first release of my book. He posed a rather powerful question that I first thought was intended for me to answer for him. But then I realized that perhaps it was rhetorical and that he was trying to answer the question himself. He wrote something to the effect of, "You've made me think a great deal about our childhood, and I have to ask, 'Where was I when all of this was taking place?'" I think he wanted to know how he missed the minutia of everyday life that I was so apt to notice. I've waited until the rerelease to answer his question in my acknowledgment page. I simply responded, "And to my brother, Eric, you were there."

3) How does your family feel about being exposed and their lives being made public?

My family hasn't really considered the magnitude of the book's potential beyond their own local environment and their circle of family and friends.

They take pride in the revelation of most of the book's content and haven't yet experienced any compromise in their own privacy. I do feel as though the book offers a historical perspective of our family and provides future generations the chance to perhaps know who we were, where we came from, and most importantly, who they may be.

4) Many authors describe writing as a transformative experience. From when you first started writing the book until the time you finished, what changes, if any, did you experience?

The one thing I did notice, ironically, was that the more I wrote about stories from my childhood or from my life, the less inclined I was to talk about them with family and friends. In other words, I felt as though I had said what I needed to say, and when people would ask me about a certain incident, situation, or quote I had noted in the book, I was less enthusiastic about discussing it. What I wanted was to talk and learn more about other stories or fond memories that were yet to be discovered or revealed. I had a desire to keep moving forward rather than backward by talking about what had been written.

5) What prompted you to begin the book? Was it something you always wanted to do?

When I moved to Los Angeles in 1995, I was basically starting my life over from scratch. I had no job, knew hardly anyone, didn't have a permanent place to live, and I had just walked away from a secure life of 401(k) plans, paid vacations, annual salary, and the corporate lifestyle for which my MBA degree had groomed me. I walked away from that security to go live and work in Hollywood. I was fortunate to get a lucky break and began working for an actor as his personal assistant. And that job led to another and to another and to another; I built a solid reputation as an assistant to celebrities, and that's no small feat. Working under pressure and managing the life of someone who lives under a microscope requires finesse, diplomacy, tact, skill, proactive inclinations, and a lot of nurturing.

I realized one day that I had acquired these talents and skills from my parents. From my childhood. And so I decided to write an extended thank-you note in the form of a book. As I was writing, I realized that I had unique commentary to offer in addition to saying thanks. Others found my style to be refreshing and grounded with an intimacy with which people could connect. I never anticipated writing this book. It has never been a life goal or aspiration. It just happened.

*6) Without doubt, you were an observant child who internal-
ized and processed the life around you. Were you exceptional?
Were other children of that time equally sensitive? Compare
children today with children of the '60s and '70s. Are there significant differences?*

I think there are significant differences between children today
and children of my generation. Of course, my parents would
have said the same when comparing children of their time
against those of mine. There's a certain degree of relativity that
accounts for some of the differences. Technology, the day and
age in which you live, and economics all impact the environment in which you live and grow. Advantages and disadvan-
tages exist because of the relative times in which you're born.
But, whereas kids today seem more advanced in terms of computer applications, technology, and advanced learning systems
and techniques, they seem to lack an instinctual awareness of
simple things about life. Their awareness of some of the basic
truths about living has been lost. I don't know that kids have a
value system remotely similar to what I had or what kids had
years and years ago.

To some degree, I was an exception even during my childhood
as I was sensitive to the world around me. More so than others. But, those others were way more intuitive, grounded, and
in-touch than kids are today. I feel fortunate that I was aware
and observant. I still am. Developing awareness takes practice
and isn't some stroke of luck. But you must be inclined or
instinctively inspired to observe and take note of life that is
happening around you. Fortunately, I was inclined to hone the
observation skill at an early age. That's what kids are missing

today. I don't see them with an interest to look at other people and the world around them.

7) You end the book by asking the reader, "And you are?" Can people define themselves in specific terms? Can you?

On a grand scale, I think people can make definite statements about who they are and what their personal constitution may be. I maintain and fully believe that a "core nucleus" exists within us, and the transference of this nucleus over time is layered with evolution, growth, change, and transition. But, the core nucleus of the basic persona exists. I can say that I'm an intuitive and compassionate person who is thankful to be able to understand people, to learn from them and their situations, and to learn from the situations I encounter as I travel through life. This has remained unchanged since my earliest memories. This will continue with me and continue to define a large part of who I am.

8) References to food are used generously throughout the book? How Southern is this inclusion? How universal?

The inclusion is absolutely Southern. Country cookin' and Southern cuisine have long defined the South by way of certain foods and styles of preparation. For example, fried foods are stereotypically associated with those of us living south of the Mason-Dixon Line, and collards and cornbread are undoubtedly devoid of any regional association other than Dixie. Food does, however, offer significant emotional comfort to so many people, regardless of geography. I'm not proposing that emotional eating is necessarily healthy; it's just comforting and has little to do with the part of the country or world in which one lives. Food is a universal way of inviting fellowship and community as well. It encourages connection among people and, in that regard, the message about food appeals to the universal palette, although it is Southern in origin.

9) In the twenty-five chapters included in Life. Be There at 10 'Til., is there one person that you can say has been the most influential in your life? And why?

It would be two people who hold equal billing as most influential: my parents, Bobby and Shirley Johnson. They taught by example as well as word. The interesting thing to note is that my parents unselfishly gave their entire lives to my brother and me. They worked hard to give to us and to help us avoid the harsh conditions of work and economic impoverishment they both knew as children. Many children might grow accustomed to such benevolence and giving and become lazy, spoiled, and unmotivated simply because someone took care of their every need. But neither my brother nor I grew to be unappreciative or unaware of the sacrifices our parents made for us. Instead, we followed their lead and learned from such selflessness. We learned by example. People often forget that the greatest gifts they can offer are the way in which they live and the examples they set for others.

10) If there were a sequel to your book, what would you write about and what would the title be?

While I'm presently writing a children's book series that offers life lessons for the much younger at heart, I would like to begin a book that focuses more on stories of my adult life outside of South Carolina. I would like to offer a comparable series of chapters that offer testament of the wisdom I've acquired as an adult. And if there were a title, I've often thought *10 Minutes Late and Still the Wiser* would be good.

One of the hardest things for me to do since writing the book has been to be on time. Life seems to have gotten busier, and my knack for overextending myself has encouraged the pattern of arriving late for meetings, social gatherings, and so forth. I always tend to show up late, and, every time I do, I think of my daddy shaking his head and wondering why I can't get to where I need to be, when I need to be there. Friends have also been quite faithful in reminding me how incongruent this habit is with the message I champion in my book. Duly noted.

Reading Group Questions and Topics for Discussion

1) In Chapter 1, Johnson sets the tone for the book by defining one's character in terms of accountability and responsibility. How appropriate are these virtues in defining character?

2) From family reunions to fellowships and funerals, it seems as though every incident in the book is an *event*—an *event* from which significant learning results. Is this Johnson's good fortune or a unique ability to discern these life lessons? Can you find wisdom in similar events from your own life? It is said that there is a book in every person. Do you think you could write a book about your experiences? What would be the title of such a collection of stories?

3) It seems as though women play a memorable and influential role in the author's life as detailed in "Birthday Girls" and "Can You Dig It?" among others. Talk about the Southern woman as heroine and icon of strength with regard to the book. Is it a regional influence (i.e., Southern) that sets these women apart? Is it more likely that these traits are more reflective of Southern women? Or, are the traits of these Southern women universal?

4) "Dear Santa" tells us that the author writes a letter to Santa every year. What did you ask for the last time you wrote to Santa? If you were to write to him today, what would you ask for?

5)   Discuss and elaborate on some of the routines you find within your daily life. Do you consider yourself a "Creature of Habit"? How do these routines comfort you? How do they inhibit you?

6)   So much of the author's childhood influences the wisdom he gained and the person he became. How much of your childhood has defined you? Has your adulthood provided more opportunity to learn and grow? Identify one instance from your childhood and one instance from your adulthood that stand out as defining moments in which you grew as a person, became wiser, or evolved.

7)   The author has admitted in the acknowledgments that his book started as an extended thank-you note to his parents. Is this book just a public thank-you or more? If you were to write a thank-you note to some influential person from your childhood, who would that person be, and what would you say?

8)   Discuss religion versus spirituality. Does the author differentiate between the two? Can you separate religion from spirituality, or are they one in the same?

9)   In such chapters as "To Cull or Not to Cull" and "A Cedar Chest and a Cubbyhole," the author touts simplicity, rather than extravagance, as a basis for having more in life—more learning, more growth, more wisdom, and more evolvement. Do you find this ironic? Is it from simplicity or bounty that people benefit?

10)   In "Lost and Found," Johnson addresses the isolation factor that is so often associated with those who are considered different or contrary to the norm—the proverbial

"black sheep," if you will. Had you lived during the time Enoch Johnson and Jayroe Dawsey did, would you have considered them to be black sheep? Do you think the author was a black sheep in any regard and why? Discuss diversity as a celebration of the human spirit.

About the Author

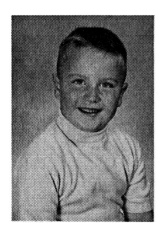 

Dawn James

South Carolina native R. Dean Johnson grew up under the stars of Southern skies and the influence of lazy accents, kind folks, good cookin', and country livin'. Yet, it was under the influence of Hollywood's stars that he grew as an author and writer. He penned the award-winning short film *Just Pray*, which was directed by actress Tiffani Thiessen, and the duo produced the narrative under their newly formed Tit 4 Tat Productions banner. Upon the picture's release in 2005, the film was accepted into the prestigious Tribeca Film Festival and Seattle International Film Festival.

Based in Los Angeles, Johnson, along with producing partner Thiessen, continues to pursue both film and television projects that offer unique storytelling opportunities. In addition,

Johnson's next literary creation is a series of children's books titled *Fins & Tales*. Thiessen joins him in crafting this collection of life lessons for the young at heart as told through the voices, hearts, and souls of her pets.

978-1-58348-232-2
1-58348-232-6

Printed in the United States
36234LVS00002B/7-15